Lecture Notes
in Economics and
Mathematical Systems
Edited by M. Beckmann, Providence, and H. P. Künzi, Zürich

Econometrics

89

J. P. Wallace · A. Sherret

Estimation of Product Attributes and Their Importances

Springer-Verlag
Berlin · Heidelberg · New York 1973

Dr. James P. Wallace III
Manager, Marketing
Systems Department, Chevrolet Motor Division, General Motors Corporation
Detroit/Michigan/USA

Dr. Alistair Sherret
Formerly Analyst, General Motors Marketing Staff; presently with Peat, Marwick, Mitchell & Co.
London, England

AMS Subject Classifications (1970): 62J10, 62P20, 90-02, 90A05, 90A15

ISBN-13: 978-3-540-06530-2 e-ISBN-13: 978-3-642-65753-5
DOI: 10.1007/978-3-642-65753-5

Offsetprinting and bookbinding: Julius Beltz, Hemsbach/Bergstr.

PREFACE

At this point in time, there is no generally accepted methodology for explaining and predicting human behavior given a product choice situation. This is true despite the critical importance of such methodology to marketing, transportation and urban planning. While the social sciences provide numerous theories to be tested and the mathematical and statistical procedures exist in general to do so, at this point, no single unified theory has emerged.

It is generally accepted that to explain product choice behavior, products must be described in terms of attributes. Using any one of a number of procedures, it is possible to obtain measurements on the attributes of the products under consideration. However, there is no generally accepted methodology.

Given the attribute profiles of two products, in order to explain and predict preference, it is necessary to determine the relative importance of each of the product attributes. Once again, there is no generally accepted methodology. There are two basic approaches: The first, called the attitudinal approach, obtains importance measurements directly from respondents using one of many scaling techniques; the second, termed the inferential method endeavors to infer importances from product preference and attribute data. Since it is generally felt that respondents are unwilling and/or unable to provide meaningful importance measurements, the inferential method is most widely accepted.

It will be argued here that the most commonly used methods of attribute measurement and of inferring attribute importances are generally invalid. Acceptance of the arguments presented here has far-reaching implications in the areas of marketing research, transportation research and other such applied fields.

The most important implication is that statistical inference models for estimating relative importances and predicting product choice behavior become much more complicated. Thus, the cost and time associated with building such models is very large.

Part I of this work discusses in some detail a proposed methodology for estimating the relative importance of product attributes via the statistical inference approach. The methodology is a systematic application of measurement theory (scaling), demand theory, generalized analysis of variance and econometrics.

Part II provides a detailed illustration of the methodology applied to the mode choice process in transportation planning. It is felt that sufficient detail is provided so that the methodology could be applied to model different product choice decisions by other interested researchers.

Numerous people have been involved in the research leading to the results reported here. However, the authors would particularly like to thank William M. Spreitzer, Head of the Transportation Research Department, General Motors Research Laboratories and Gail Smith, General Director, Advertising and Merchandising, General Motors Corporation for their support of this research.

The authors would also like to express their appreciation to Professors Martin Beckmann, Marc Nerlove and Francesco Nicosia for their comments and suggestions on early drafts of this work. However, errors remaining should be attributed solely to the authors.

CONTENTS

PART I. Estimating the Relative Importance of Product Attributes

1. Introduction

One of the most fundamental questions that arises in both advertising and product planning is what product attributes (i.e., characteristics) are most important in the consumer decision making process. Advertising objectives are often set based on improving consumer perception of a product in terms of the specific product attributes deemed to be most important.[1] In the product planning area, decisions must always be made which require trade-offs in that a higher level of one attribute necessitates a lower (or higher) level of some other attribute due to engineering and/or financial considerations. These trade-off decisions require inputs regarding the relative importance consumers attach to the attributes in question.[2]

To be of assistance in these decisions, the marketing analyst must first obtain measures on a set of attributes that describes the alternative products from a consumer choice point of view. The analyst must then determine which product attributes appear to be most important to consumers in their choice between alternative products. However, while there is a great deal of literature which is relevant, there is no generally accepted methodology. A full review of this literature is not possible here, but Myers and Alpert and others have provided a review of many of the various approaches that have been

---

[1] David A. Schwartz, "Measuring the Effectiveness of Your Company's Advertising," *Journal of Marketing*, Vol. 33 (April, 1969), pp. 20-25.

[2] James P. Wallace III, "Some Applications of Marketing Research Techniques to the New Mode Demand Forecasting Problem," *Selected Proceedings of a Conference on Methods and Concepts of Forecasting Travel Demand for Future Transportation Systems* (Transportation Studies Center, Center for Urban Research and Experiment, University of Pennsylvania, Philadelphia, Pennsylvania, April, 1972).

suggested.[3] The purpose of this work then is to develop and illustrate a new approach for obtaining measures on a set of attributes that describes alternative products from a consumer viewpoint and for estimating the relative importance consumers attach to each of the attributes in selecting between the alternative products.

The particular consumer product choice selected to illustrate the methodology suggested is the transportation mode (product) choice decision for the journey to work. In this case, the choice involved is between the automobile and rail transit. However, Wallace, in an earlier paper, has applied some of the same methodology for new car purchase decisions with encouraging results.[4] The approach suggested here is, generally speaking, a combined application of measurement theory (scaling), consumer demand theory, generalized analysis of variance and econometrics.

2. Attribute Definition and Measurement

Developing a description of alternative products in terms of attributes immediately raises the problem of definition and measurement. "Quantitative Attributes," that is, those with natural physical units of measurement familiar to the consumer, cause little difficulty. Examples are price ($) and gas mileage (miles/gallon) for automobiles or travel time (minutes) and fare ($) for modes of travel. But "qualitative attributes" having no natural physical unit of measurement familiar to the consumer do cause a problem. Examples are tartness and cleaning power for toothpaste, comfort, sex appeal, dependability and noise for automobiles. Since in practice it is seldom (if ever) possible to fully describe alternative products solely in terms of quantitative attributes, some scaling technique is required. It will later

[3] James H. Myers and Mark I. Alpert, "Determining Buying Attitudes: Meaning and Measurement," Journal of Marketing, Vol. 32 (October, 1968), pp. 13-20.

[4] James P. Wallace III and Ralph L. Miller, "Consumer Behavior Models for the Automotive Market" (Presented at the Operations' Research Convention, San Francisco, 1968).

be argued that since this is so, for consistency it seems reasonable to obtain scale ratings on all attributes.

There is considerable literature on scaling procedures and their applications. There are the traditional metric methods such as the semantic differential, the Thurstone methods and the newer non-metric scaling methods. Each has its strengths and weaknesses, a discussion of which is beyond the scope of this paper. Green and Tull provide a thorough review of these methods.[5] The approach taken here is the semantic differential, but other procedures could have been used. However, a recent study by Green and Rao indicates that the traditional metric scaling techniques appear to perform as well as the newer non-metric methods when it comes to returning a known product group configuration.[6]

Product attribute definition and measurement via the semantic differential requires, first, a choice as to the number of intervals; second, a selection of polar adjectives to define the end points of the scale; and third, a choice between a monadic and paired comparison research design. A seven point scale has been recommended by Osgood.[7] While some have suggested fewer intervals, the Green and Rao work also supports Osgood's recommendation -- so that selecting a seven point scale appears reasonable.[8]

---

[5]Paul E. Green and Donald S. Tull, Research for Marketing Decisions, (Prentice-Hall, Inc., Englewood Cliffs, New Jersey, 1970).

[6]Paul E. Green and Vithala R. Rao, "Rating Scales and Information Recovery - How Many Scales and Response Categories to Use?" Journal of Marketing, Vol. 34 (July, 1970), pp. 33-39.

[7]Charles E. Osgood, George J. Suci and Percy H. Tannenbaum, The Measurement of Meaning (University of Illinois Press, Urbana, Illinois, 1957).

[8]Green and Rao, pp. 33-39.

Regarding the definition of polar adjectives, there appear to be two approaches. The first is to attempt to define the end points so that attribute rating measurements will not be "value loaded," that is, depend solely on the level of the attribute and are not dependent on the respondent's utility function.[9] But for qualitative attributes in particular, this does not appear to be possible since it is very difficult (if not impossible) to define end points which guarantee that most respondents do not provide ratings based on a mental comparison with other actual or ideal products. Assuming this is the case, the only alternative is to force value loaded judgments from respondents by appropriate selection of the polar adjectives. In this way, individual measurements become attribute satisfaction ratings rather than attribute ratings since respondents are asked to provide a measure of their satisfaction with regard to a particular attribute of a specific product.

Models are often formulated in which attribute ratings and attribute satisfaction ratings are used interchangeably. A regression model is cited in Myers and Alpert wherein certain attributes of a cocktail mix dip such as color, overall appearance and taste were rated on a seven point scale with end points "liked very much" and "disliked very much;" whereas other attributes such as strength of flavor and spiciness were rated on a five point scale from "much too strong (spicy)" to "much too weak (bland)."[10] Buying intention was used as the dependent variable. Note that attribute satisfaction ratings were obtained on the first set of attributes whereas there was an apparent attempt to obtain attribute ratings on the latter set. A more obvious attempt would have been to label the end points "very weak" to "very strong"

---

[9] Hope S. Roman, "Semantic Generalization in Formation of Consumer Attitudes," Journal of Marketing Research, Vol. VI (August, 1969), pp. 369-373.

[10] Myers and Alpert, p. 18.

for flavor and "very spicy" to "very bland" for spiciness. However, even with these end points, some respondents will, in general, provide ratings based on a mental comparison with another actual or ideal product in the same choice category, while other respondents may provide ratings which are not value loaded. This inconsistency among respondents leads to unreliable measurements and strongly suggests the use of end point definitions which clearly request measures of satisfaction with a particular product attribute. This implies the use of end points such as "poor/excellent," "very unsatisfactory/very satisfactory" or "highly unsatisfactory/completely acceptable." See, for example, Table I. Although of critical importance, it is beyond the scope of this paper to argue this point further.

The fact that it does not appear possible to obtain reliable measures regarding the level of qualitative attributes necessitating the measurement of attribute satisfaction ratings has very important ramifications when it comes to building models to estimate the importance of attributes. This arises due to the fact that attribute satisfaction ratings depend on both the level of the attribute (not directly measureable for qualitative attributes) and the individual consumer's utility function whereas utility functions are normally specified in terms of product attributes.[11] A potential solution to this problem was suggested by Wallace, and a questionnaire was designed to provide the data necessary to calibrate and validate the proposed consumer choice model.[12] The data obtained and method of collection is described in Section 3 below.

As stated above, a choice must also be made between a paired com-

---

[11] Kelvin J. Lancaster, "A New Approach to Consumer Theory," Journal of Political Economy, Vol. 74 (April, 1966), pp. 132-157.

[12] Wallace, "Some Applications of Marketing Research Techniques to the New Mode Demand Forecasting Problem."

parison or a monadic research design. Greenberg's study provides numerous references regarding the strengths and weaknesses of the two approaches.[13] One of the major arguments against the paired comparison approach is that it tends to magnify what are actually minor differences in attribute satisfaction. This problem is particularly relevant when these data are to be used as input to a model designed to infer the importance of attributes from consumer product choice decisions. Another strong argument in favor of the monadic design is that it provides data in the case of quantitative attributes, to test alternative hypotheses regarding the mapping from attributes to attribute satisfaction ratings. This fact will be made use of in Section 10. Because of these points, a monadic design appears most reasonable. Of course, the monadic design must be used if an attribute has a different meaning or no meaning at all for one of the products under consideration.

3. The Experiment

As mentioned above, the product choice decision process for which data were collected is the journey to work/mode choice decision. The following information was obtained via a five page, mailed questionnaire for the respondent's first and second choice mode: attribute satisfaction ratings based on the semantic differential for 15 different attributes (see Table I), attribute values on seven quantitative attributes (see Table II) and the usual demographic data. There was a total mailing of 10,000; approximately 1,000 were returned. The statistical results in this paper are for the subsample making the choice auto (driver or passenger) versus rail transit. The total sample was 117 (60 choosing auto, 57, transit). A detailed discussion of the questionnaire and its design is in the literature.[14]

---

[13] Allen Greenberg, "Paired Comparisons Versus Monadic Tests," Journal of Advertising Research, Vol. 3, No. 4 (December, 1963), pp. 44-47.

[14] Thomas F. Golob, The Survey of User Choice of Alternate Transportation Modes, Research Publication GMR-950 (General Motors Research Laboratories, Warren, Michigan, January, 1970).

TABLE I

ATTRIBUTE SATISFACTION RATINGS

Below is a list of phrases some people use to describe their trip to work. For each phrase, rate your overall HOME TO WORK trip by placing a check mark ☑ in the box along the scale at that point which best describes your SATISFACTION with that aspect of the overall trip. If a phrase does not apply, check the box marked "Not Applicable" (N.A.)

No.	Attribute		Scale		N.A.
1.	COMFORT IN VEHICLE *(See Footnote)	EXCELLENT	[7][6][5][4][3][2][1]	POOR	[0]
2.	DEPENDABILITY OF ON-TIME ARRIVAL	EXCELLENT	☐☐☐☐☐☐☐	POOR	☐
3.	PROTECTION FROM WEATHER WHILE WAITING	EXCELLENT	☐☐☐☐☐☐☐	POOR	☐
4.	FREQUENCY OF VEHICLE DEPARTURE TIMES	EXCELLENT	☐☐☐☐☐☐☐	POOR	☐
5.	PLEASANTNESS OF TRIP	EXCELLENT	☐☐☐☐☐☐☐	POOR	☐
6.	ATTRACTIVENESS OF VEHICLE *(See Footnote)	EXCELLENT	☐☐☐☐☐☐☐	POOR	☐
7.	NOISE IN VEHICLE *(See Footnote)	COMPLETELY ACCEPTABLE	☐☐☐☐☐☐☐	HIGHLY UNSATISFACTORY	☐
8.	CHANCE OF ACCIDENTS	COMPLETELY ACCEPTABLE	☐☐☐☐☐☐☐	HIGHLY UNSATISFACTORY	☐
9.	EXPOSURE TO UNDESIRABLE BEHAVIOR OF OTHERS	COMPLETELY ACCEPTABLE	☐☐☐☐☐☐☐	HIGHLY UNSATISFACTORY	☐
10.	TRAFFIC	COMPLETELY ACCEPTABLE	☐☐☐☐☐☐☐	HIGHLY UNSATISFACTORY	☐
11.	BODILY CROWDING	COMPLETELY ACCEPTABLE	☐☐☐☐☐☐☐	HIGHLY UNSATISFACTORY	☐
12.	OUT OF POCKET COST OF TRIP	COMPLETELY ACCEPTABLE	☐☐☐☐☐☐☐	HIGHLY UNSATISFACTORY	☐
13.	TOTAL TIME SPENT RIDING	COMPLETELY ACCEPTABLE	☐☐☐☐☐☐☐	HIGHLY UNSATISFACTORY	☐
14.	TOTAL TIME SPENT WALKING	COMPLETELY ACCEPTABLE	☐☐☐☐☐☐☐	HIGHLY UNSATISFACTORY	☐
15.	TOTAL TIME SPENT WAITING	COMPLETELY ACCEPTABLE	☐☐☐☐☐☐☐	HIGHLY UNSATISFACTORY	☐

(Consider vehicle used for LONGEST TIME during trip)

TABLE II

KEY TO ATTRIBUTE DESCRIPTIONS
(Quantitative Attributes Only)

Attribute Number	Description	Units	Abbreviation
4	Vehicle Interdeparture Times	minutes	Frequency
13	Total Time Spent Riding	minutes	Riding Time
14	Total Time Spent Walking	minutes	Walking Time
15	Total Time Spent Waiting	minutes	Waiting Time
16	Distance Travelled	miles(coded)	Distance
17	Daily Parking Cost	cents	Parking Cost
18	One-way Fare	cents	Fare

4. Demand Equation Formulation and Estimation Procedures

The first objective of this section is to develop the demand side of a model for estimating the importance of product attributes. Actually a family of demand side equations are developed. The second objective is to suggest means by which these models can be estimated. To facilitate later discussion of the empirical results, the model will be described in terms of the mode choice decision. To generalize, replace traveller by consumer and mode by product.

The model will confine itself to explaining the modal choice behavior of individuals who actually do have a choice between alternatives (i.e., are not "captive" to any one mode), and will consider the modal choice as a binary decision between the two "best" alternatives available. The latter assumption is based simply on the hypothesis that the typical traveller is unlikely to have many more than two feasible alternatives and that in any case in the end is not likely to make a decision between more than two; that is, he is likely to reduce a choice between three or more to the "best" two and choose between these. This process of reducing the number of alternatives as the time of actual choice nears is discussed by Nicosia and others.[15]

Now establish the following notation: For a representative individual traveller from the population, for modes $j = 1,2$ and attributes $i = 1,2...,m$;

y probability that mode 1 is preferred to mode 2

X_i^j value or level of attribute i on mode j

X^j m-element vector of attribute values $\left[X_i^j\right]$ for mode j

$Q_i^j = Q_i(X_i^j)$ attribute satisfaction rating for attribute value X_i^j

Q^j m-element vector of attribute satisfaction ratings $\left[Q_i^j\right]$

$Q_i = Q_i(X_i^1) - Q_i(X_i^2) = Q_i^1 - Q_i^2$

relative attribute satisfaction rating for attribute i for modes 1 and 2

Q m-element vector of relative attribute satisfaction ratings $\left[Q_i\right]$

$U_i(X_i^j)$ utility associated with attribute value X_i^j

$U(X^j)$ total utility associated with mode j

Next, assume the probability that an individual chooses mode 1, that is, prefers mode 1 to mode 2, is a function f of the difference in the total utilities to him of the two modes.

4.1) $y = f\ (\ U(X^1)\ -\ U(X^2))$

The probability p that he prefers mode 2 to mode 1 is then assumed to be

4.2) $p = 1 - y$

indicating that a choice is made to travel by either mode 1 or mode 2. Generalizing to the choice between many modes is non-trivial.

Also assume the total utility of a mode is derived from the

[15] Francesco Nicosia, Consumer Decision Processes (Prentice-Hall, Inc., Englewood Cliffs, New Jersey, 1966), pp. 215-220.

utilities of the attributes of the mode in the additive form

4.3) $$U(X^j) = \sum_{i=1}^{m} U_i(X_i^j) \qquad j = 1,2$$

The assumption of "additive utilities," i.e., the assumption that the utility of the whole is equal to the sum of the utilities of its parts, is an important one in the model formulation because of its implication that the attributes are valuewise independent. Thus, for equation (4.3) to be valid, the utility $U(X_i^j)$ must be independent of X_k^j for all $k \neq i$. Fishburn, for example, in the context of the factors determining the utility of a decision states this as the requirement that the "evaluator be able to make consistent value judgments about the levels of any one factor when the levels of all other factors are held fixed, and his judgments must not depend on the particular fixed levels of the other factors."[16] This assumption implies the desirability of developing a set of attributes which fully describes the products under consideration that from a consumer point of view can be measured along orthogonal axes. This is discussed further in Section 8.

Combining equations (4.1) and 4.3)

4.4 $$y = f\left(\sum_{i=1}^{m} \left[U_i(X_i^1) - U_i(X_i^2) \right] \right)$$

Note that the function $U_i(X_i^j)$, it is assumed, is not dependent on the mode j (although obviously is dependent on the attribute i). That is to say, the utility derived from a certain value of some attribute, say travel time, is the same whether this is the travel time by bus or by automobile. This assumption is to some extent validated in Section 10.

Next, assume that the function $U_i(X_i^j)$ is monotonic in X_i^j and has the diminishing marginal utility property (as is commonly assumed as the basis for theories of rational economic behavior of consumers).

---

[16] Peter C. Fishburn, "Methods of Estimating Additive Utilities," Management Science, Vol. 13, No. 7 (1967), P. 436.

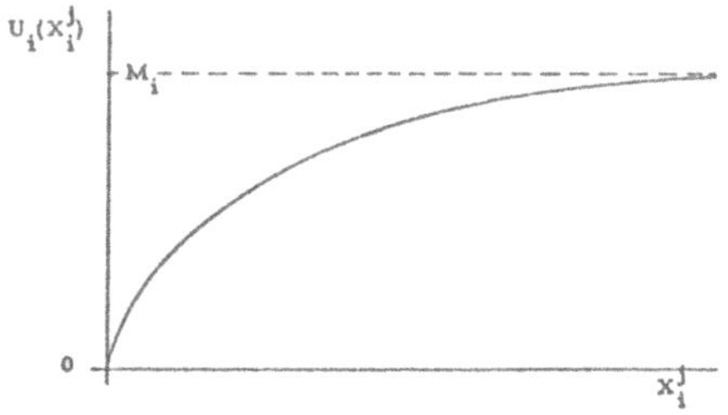

fig. 4.1

The form of fig. 4.1 is appropriate where high attribute values or levels are associated with high levels of utility, for instance comfort, dependability, safety. Attributes having an associated utility function of this form can be referred to as "comfort-type" attributes.

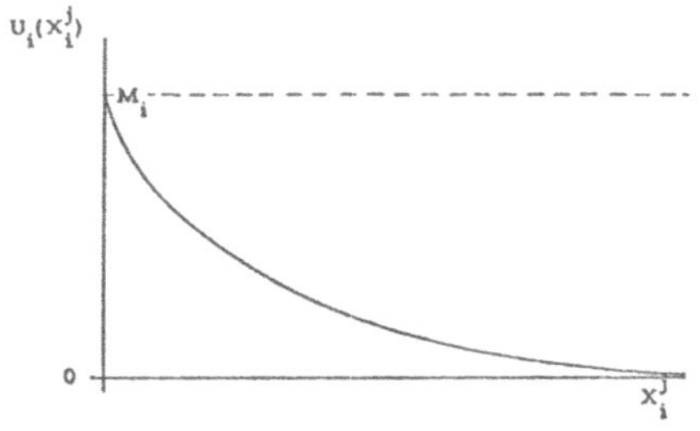

fig. 4.2

The form of fig. 4.2 is appropriate for what may be termed "cost-type" attributes, i.e., those for which high values of the attribute are associated with low levels of utility such as cost of travel. The value of M_i is the maximum level of utility associated by the traveller with any value or level of the attribute, and obviously the value of M_i will not, in general, be the same for different attributes i. Note, however, that it is assumed not dependent on the mode j and is assumed to be finite.

The relationships depicted in figures 4.1 and 4.2 are assumed to be of the form

4.5) $\quad U_i(X_i^j) = M_i \; h_i(X_i^j)$

A specific form for $h_i(X_i^j)$ which seems reasonable is the exponential

4.6) $h_i(X_i^j) = (1 - e^{-\lambda_i X_i^j})$ for comfort-type attributes i and

4.7) $h_i(X_i^j) = e^{-\lambda_i X_i^j}$ for cost-type attributes i.

These assumptions make it possible to specify the demand equation (4.4) in terms of the attribute values X_i^j. However, X_i^j is not measurable (see section 2) for qualitative attributes so that the demand equation must be written in terms of Q_i, the attribute satisfaction ratings.

Let the attribute satisfaction rating $Q_i(X_i^j)$ be measured on a semantic differential scale with (k + 1) scale intervals 0,1,...,k, and assume the following direct proportionality relationship between $Q_i(X_i^j)$ and $U_i(X_i^j)$

4.8) $Q_i(X_i^j)/k = U_i(X_i^j)/M_i$

where M_i is the maximum utility associated with attribute i, which may be illustrated for, say, a cost-type attribute with K = 6 (a seven point scale) as shown in Figure 4.3.

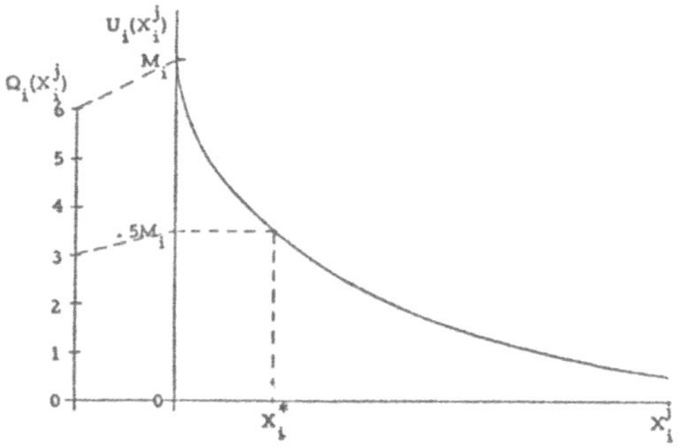

fig. 4.3

Combining equations (4.5) and (4.8) and writing Q_i^j for $Q_i(X_i^j)$

4.9) $Q_i^j = k\, h(X_i^j)$

Also note here that if the semantic differential scale does not have a zero origin, then appropriate adjustments must be made. If, for instance, a k-point scale 1,2,...,K is utilized (as is the case for this data) the relationships (and their inverses) for the exponential form of $h(X_i^j)$ in equations (4.6) and (4.7) are respectively:

4.10) $Q_i^j = 1 + (k - 1)(1 - e^{-\lambda_i X_i^j})$ for comfort-type attributes

4.11) $Q_i^j = 1 + (k - 1)\, e^{-\lambda_i X_i^j}$ for cost-type attributes

4.12) $X_i^j = \frac{1}{\lambda_i} \log((k - 1)/(k - Q_i^j))$ for comfort-type attributes

4.13) $X_i^j = \frac{1}{\lambda_i} \log((k - 1)/(Q_i^j - 1))$ for cost-type attributes

Finally, note that the "Q/X" relationships hypothesized in, say, equations (4.10) and (4.11) above may be estimated and their validity investigated for those attributes for which a sample of observations on both attribute values and the corresponding attribute satisfaction ratings is available. The results of this investigation are reported in Section 10 and are quite encouraging.

Now, combine the demand equation (4.4) with equation (4.8) to obtain the demand equation

4.14) $$y = f\left(\frac{1}{k} \sum_{i=1}^{m} M_i \left[Q_i(X_i^1) - Q_i(X_i^2)\right]\right)$$

The variable $Q_i(X_i^1) - Q_i(X_i^2)$ (or $Q_i^1 - Q_i^2$) is the difference in the attribute satisfaction ratings (measured on the same semantic differential scale) for attribute i. In order to simplify notation, this variable will be written as Q_i and referred to as the <u>relative attribute satisfaction rating</u> for attribute i. The m-element vector of relative attribute satisfaction ratings $[Q_i]$ will be written as Q. Equation (4.14) may then be written as

4.15) $$y = f\left(\frac{1}{k} \sum_{i=1}^{m} M_i Q_i\right)$$

or more concisely as

4.16) $y = f(Q)$

Any one of a number of forms may be proposed for the function f, the more straightforward being included in the class of functions h such that $f(Q) = h(g(Q))$ and where $g(Q)$ is a linear function of the Q_i

4.17) $g(Q) = a_0 + \sum_{i=1}^{m} a_i Q_i$

where $a_i = M_i/k$. The following discussion will be confined to this class of functions. Most simple of this class is the case where h is the identity function so that

4.18) $f(Q) = g(Q)$

and

4.19) $y = a_0 + \sum_{i=1}^{m} a_i Q_i$

This has been referred to as the linear probability function.

Suppose (as is the case here) observations on the dependent variable y are dichotomous taking on the value one if the individual prefers mode 1 and zero if mode 2. This raises peculiar problems of estimation which have been considered, for instance, by Warner[17] and Goldberger[18]. It is possible to treat (4.19) as a classical linear regression model with the expected value of the regressand (the dependent variable) y specified as a linear function of nonstochastic regressors (explanatory variables) Q_i, and obtain classical least squares estimates of the parameters. The conditional expectation of y may then be interpreted as the conditional probability of modal choice given the

---

[17] Stanley L. Warner, Stochastic Choice of Mode in Urban Travel: A Study in Binary Choice (Northwestern University Press, Evanston, Illinois, 1962).

[18] Arthur S. Goldberger, Econometric Theory (John Wiley & Sons, Inc., New York, 1964) pp. 248-251.

Q_i. As shown by Goldberger, however, the basic classical least squares assumption of homoskedasticity is not fulfilled in the case of a "dummy" dependent variable, since the disturbance term of the model varies systematically with the values of the regressors. Consequently, the classical least squares estimates although unbiased are inefficient.[19] Classical least squares estimation of (4.19) does not then yield "best" estimates of the coefficients. However, it should be mentioned that the heteroskedasticity problem can be alleviated by obtaining a probability of choice measure from respondents over the interval ($0 \leq p \leq 1$).

Moreover, in addition to the difficulty caused by heteroskedasticity, the linear probability function of (4.19) itself may be objected to on the grounds that it is quite possible for predicted values of y to fall outside the 0,1 interval, which is inconsistent with the definition of y as a probability. The function is thus "illogical at the ends."

Two methods have been widely used to take care of the problem of confining predicted values of the regressand to the unit interval. These are probit analysis and logit analysis, both of which essentially fit an S-shaped "sigmoid" curve to a linear function of the data. Denoting g(Q) as the linear function, the general form of the sigmoid curve fitted by probit and logit analysis is as given in fig. 4.4.

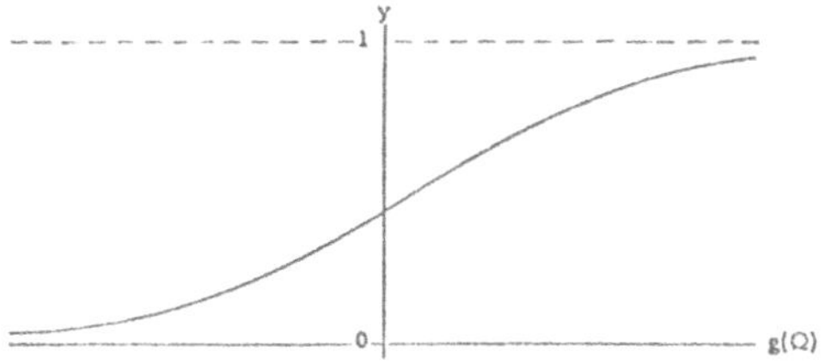

fig. 4.4

In probit analysis the sigmoid function is given by the cumulative normal distribution function

4.20) $$y = \frac{1}{\sqrt{2\pi}} \int_{-\infty}^{g(Q)} e^{-t^2/2}\, dt$$

[19]Goldberger, p. 238.

where $g(Q) = a_0 + \sum_{i=1}^{m} a_i Q_i$

Non-Linear estimation yields maximum liklihood estimates of the parameters of g(Q) as shown by Tobin.[20]

Logit analysis, which like probit has its origins in bio-assay,[21] fits the logistic curve to a linear function g(Q).

4.21) $$y = \frac{1}{1 + e^{-g(Q)}}$$

where $g(Q) = a_0 + \sum_{i=1}^{m} a_i Q_i$

For both probit and logit analysis, assuming the usual assumptions hold, maximum likelihood estimates of the parameters of the linear function g(Q) may be obtained which are both unbiased and efficient. No conclusive evidence has been presented to indicate that statistically one provides a better fit than the other to modal choice data.[22]

Here the demand equation will be estimated by three methods. First, because of its computational simplicity, ordinary least squares regression is used to estimate the linear probability function of (4.19). Second, using non-linear least squares regression, the logistic function of (4.21) is estimated.[23] Third, the demand equation is estimated as an integral part of a system of equations via two-stage least squares.

---

[20] James Tobin, The Application of Multivariate Probit Analysis to Economic Survey Data, Cowles Foundation Discussion Paper No. 1 (New Haven, Connecticut, December, 1955).

[21] Joseph Berkson, "A Statistically Precise and Relatively Simple Method of Estimating the Bio-Assay with Quantal Response, Based on the Logistic Function," Journal of the American Statistical Association, Vol. 48, No. 263 (1953), pp. 565-599.

[22] Warner, pp. 20-21.

[23] H. O. Hartley, "The Modified Gauss-Newton Method for the Fitting of Non-Linear Regression Functions by Least Squares," Technometrics, Vol. 3, No. 3 (1961), pp. 269-280.

5. Demand Equation Parameter Interpretation as Importances

Next, the concept of importance will be discussed and then defined in the context of the consumer choice model described above. As has been pointed out by Myers and Alpert, the term importance has been used to mean many different things. It is necessary, therefore, to define carefully what is to be meant by importance here. From the point of view of the consumer, the relative importance of attributes can be said to be the ratio of the marginal utilities of attributes, that is

5.1) $$\frac{dU_i}{dX_i} \bigg/ \frac{dU_m}{dX_m} \quad \text{or} \quad \frac{dU_i}{dQ_i} \bigg/ \frac{dU_m}{dQ_m} \qquad (i = 1,2,\ldots,m-1)$$

depending on whether the utility function is specified in terms of attribute or attribute satisfaction ratings. From the point of view of allocating advertising funds or funds for product change, attribute importance may be defined differently. Letting C equal dollar expenditure; importance in this case is given by:

5.2) $$\frac{dU_i}{dX_i} \quad \frac{dX_i}{dC} \bigg/ \frac{dU_m}{dX_m} \quad \frac{dX_m}{dC} \qquad (i = 1,2,\ldots,m-1) \text{ or}$$

5.3) $$\frac{dU_i}{dQ_i} \quad \frac{dQ_i}{dC} \bigg/ \frac{dU_m}{dQ_m} \quad \frac{dQ_m}{dC} \qquad (i = 1,2,\ldots,m-1)$$

since it is assumed that preference and therefore sales, is monotonic in U. Note that, given the additive utility assumption, total rather than partial derivatives are appropriate.

Methods for estimating dX/dC for quantitative attributes and dQ/dC for all attributes are outside the scope of this paper. Suffice it to say that, in the case of advertising planning, advertising pretesting procedures can be used and, in the case of product development, product clinic procedures can be applied. In the case of quantitative attributes, care must be taken to note that the model is in terms of perceived attributes not actual attributes so that engineering and financial estimates may not suffice.

In order to obtain comparable importance measures for all attributes, it seems reasonable to obtain semantic differential attribute satisfaction ratings for all attributes, even those which are quantitative. As a result attribute importances defined in terms of Q rather than X will be considered.

Of primary interest here then is dU_i/dQ_i ($i = 1, 2, \ldots, m$). But differentiation of equation (4.8) implies that

$$5.4) \quad \frac{dU_i}{dQ_i} = \frac{M_i}{k} = a_i \qquad (i = 1,2,\ldots,m)$$

in equation (4.17). Thus, based on the assumption leading to equation (4.8) relative importance from a consumer viewpoint is given by

$$5.5) \quad \frac{a_i}{a_m} = \frac{M_i}{M_m} \qquad (i = 1,2,\ldots,m)$$

As a result the demand model(s) given by equation(s) (4.15) imply that preference depends on relative attribute satisfaction ratings and attribute importances. A validation of assumption (4.8) is provided in Section 10. Means by which the a_i can be estimated have been discussed above and results will be given below.

The hypothesis that attitude and consequently behavior are determined by the satisfaction with, and importance of, the "attitude object" has been the basis for attitudinal models in applied psychology.

Fishbein has suggested an additive utility model which implies that an individual's attitude toward an object will depend on (1) how satisfactorily the object possesses certain attributes, and (2) how important these attributes are to him.[24] Confirmation of hypotheses of

---

[24] M. Fishbein, Readings in Attitude Theory and Measurement (John Wiley & Sons, Inc., New York, 1967).

this kind suggests that the choice behavior of individuals can be described in terms of their satisfaction with the perceived level of modal attributes and the importance attached by them to the attributes. Bass and Talarzyk have utilized this approach in their research.[25] Frequently "importances" are estimated via regression techniques and discriminant analysis.[26]

There are, therefore, precedents for this modal choice formulation. Note, however, that this model, in contrast to the psychological models discussed above, involves no a priori specifications of the coefficients as importances. The interpretation instead arises naturally as a direct consequence of the model assumptions of 1) additive utilities, 2) the particular diminishing marginal utility form of the utility function and 3) the proportional mapping from U to Q. As mentioned previously the latter two assumptions are validated in Section 10.

6. Supply Side Formulation

To this point the consumer choice model has been expressed in terms of a single demand equation, and in the preceding section, it was shown that estimation of the parameters of the equation would yield estimates of the relative importances of the associated attributes. However, the data which must be used to estimate the model was "generated" by the simultaneous solution of demand and supply relationships. Estimation of the single equation demand model from such data, while ignoring the supply side, is consequently likely to yield statistically biased and inconsistent estimates of the relative importances, and these estimates may be misleading.[27] It will be shown in Section 12 that this

---

[25] F. M. Bass and W. W. Talarzyk, "A Study of Attitude Theory and Brand Preference" (Presented at the American Marketing Associate Educators Conference, Fall, 1969).

[26] H. J. Einhoin, "The Use of Nonlinear, Noncompensatory Models in Decision Making" (Unpublished Doctoral Dissertation, Wayne State University, Detroit, Michigan, 1969).

[27] Goldberger, pp. 280-290.

turned out to be the case in the illustrative example cited here. In order to obtain meaningful estimates of importances, the relevant supply side relationships must be included in the structure of the model, and the model must be estimated via one of the techniques appropriate for estimating systems of simultaneous equations. A discussion of these techniques is outside the scope of this paper. Goldberger provides an excellent reference textbook.[28]

It is important to note that even though the data is taken via questioning the traveller, for each of the two modes considered, certain of the attribute values are related to other attribute values because of supply considerations. Suppose that for mode j some of these supply considerations can be expressed by an equation relating the value of attribute r to the values of other attributes i. Simple equation forms which may be thought appropriate for specific supply relationships are, for instance, the additive form

6.1) $$X_r^j = b_r^j + \sum_i b_i^j X_i^j$$

or the multiplicative form

6.2) $$X_r^j = b_r^j \prod_i b_i^j X_i^j$$

where the b are coefficients to be estimated. The additive form may be, for example, appropriate for the automobile mode for, say, a relationship describing the value of the attribute "out-of-pocket cost" as an additive function of the various other attributes such as traffic, travel time and parking costs. Any number of other more complex equation forms may, of course, be hypothesized; these two are suggested only as possible simple forms. Moreover, as before, some of the attribute values X_i^j may be difficult or impossible to measure, in which case it is necessary to resort to the use of the corresponding attribute

[28] Goldberger, Econometric Theory

satisfaction ratings Q_i^j in estimating the relationships.

Assume the first p of the "right-hand side" attributes $i = 1,\ldots,p$ of equations (6.1) and (6.2) are expressed in terms of their satisfaction ratings ("Q" variables) and the next q, $i = p + 1,\ldots,p + q$ are expressed in terms of attribute values ("X" variables). Also let the left-hand attribute r be expressed as a satisfaction rating.

As before, assume that the exponential relationships given by equations (4.12) and (4.13) exist between X_i^j and Q_i^j $i = 1,\ldots,p,r$ so that

6.3) $$X_i^j = \frac{1}{\lambda_i} \log ((k - 1)/Q_i^{j*})$$

where $Q_i^{j*} = (Q_i^j - 1)$ for cost-type attributes

and $Q_i^{j*} = (k - Q_i^j)$ for comfort-type attributes.

Substituting for X_i^j $i = 1,\ldots,p,r$ from (6.3) in the equation (6.1) then yields one possible form of supply relationship:

6.4) $$Q_r^{j*} = \prod_{i=1}^{p} (Q_i^{j*})^{c_i^j} \exp (c_r^j + \sum_{i=p+1}^{p+q} c_i^j X_i^j)$$

The coefficients c are simple arithmetic combinations of the coefficients b, λ, and k.

Suppose the exponential relationships of (6.3) may be approximated by a linear relationship over the ranges of X_i^j and Q_i^j of interest, viz.

6.5) $$X_i^j = \mu_{0i} + \mu_i Q_i^j$$

This form also results from assuming U to be a linear function of X. Substituting for X_i^j $i = 1,\ldots,p,r$ in equation (6.1) then yields another possible form of supply side relationship:

6.6) $$Q_r^j = c_0^j + \sum_{i=1}^{p} c_i^j Q_i^j + \sum_{i=p+1}^{p+q} c_i^j X_i^j .$$

where, again, the coefficients c are simply derived from the coefficients of (6.1) and (6.5). It should be stressed that the supply side equations (6.4) and (6.6) which are derived above are only suggested as possible forms of supply side relationships which have some plausibility and are relatively simple to estimate. They will be referred to as the "nonlinear" and "linear" supply equations respectively. It is important to note that attributes included in the demand equation may be correlated due to correlation with a third variable rather than due to direct causal relationships.

The two tables below show the correlation between semantic differential ratings of dependability (1) out-of-pocket cost (2) riding time (3) walking time (4) and waiting time (5) for auto and transit.

CORRELATION MATRIX — AUTO

	1	2	3	4	5
Dependability	1.0000				
Cost	0.3303	1.0000			
Riding Time	0.5855	0.4429	1.0000		
Walking Time	0.0671	0.0232	-0.0429	1.0000	
Waiting Time	0.2618	0.1585	0.2871	-0.0425	1.0000

CORRELATION MATRIX — TRANSIT

	1	2	3	4	5
Dependability	1.0000				
Cost	0.4545	1.0000			
Riding Time	0.4463	0.4746	1.0000		
Walking Time	0.1560	0.2328	0.2468	1.0000	
Waiting Time	0.7252	0.3880	0.4615	0.3765	1.0000

For the automobile, relatively high correlations exist between dependability and riding time as well as out-of-pocket cost and riding time due to supply side considerations. Supply side relationships were developed involving these variables as well as dependability and waiting time for transit. It is beyond the scope of this work to develop these equations here. However, for this mode choice problem supply side model development has been given by Sherret[29] and will be further discussed in Part II.

7. Simultaneous Equation Model Formulation

Having discussed the demand side and supply side relationships, it is now possible to propose a simple simultaneous model structure. Assume for purposes of illustration that both the demand and supply relationship are linear; more complex equation forms (in the same variables) may be substituted without changing the basic structure of the model. Then

7.1) $$y = a_0 + \sum_{i=1}^{m} a_i Q_i$$

where

7.2) $$Q_i = Q_i^1 - Q_i^2 \qquad i = 1,\ldots,m$$

and

7.3) $$Q_i^j = c_{0i}^j + \sum_{k=1}^{p} c_{ki}^j Q_k^j + \sum_{k=p+1}^{p+q} c_{ki}^j X_k^j \qquad \begin{matrix} i = 1,\ldots,m \\ j = 1,2 \end{matrix}$$

Equation (7.1) is the demand relationship expressing the probability of modal choice in terms of the relative attribute satisfaction variables Q_i, with the coefficients a_i, $i = 1,\ldots,m$ being the importances of the modal attributes which are to be estimated. Equation set (7.2) is simply a set of identities defining the relative attribute

---

[29]Alistair Sherret, "Structuring an Econometric Model of Mode Choice" (Dissertation: Cornell University, 1971).

satisfaction ratings Q_i as the difference in attribute satisfaction ratings for mode 1 minus mode 2. These identities provide the link with the supply side relationships of the equations (7.3) which express for modes 1 and 2 separately the relationships existing between the attributes of the modes on the supply side. Equations (7.3) indicate that there exist supply relationships for all the m attributes of both modes 1 and 2. While this may be true in general, it is likely that in any given model formulation some of the Q_i^j will be considered exogenous to the model -- in each of which cases the coefficients of all the variables on the right-hand side of the relevant supply relationship will be zero with the exception of the particular Q_i^j for which the coefficient is one.

In the model the variable y and all those Q_i^j for which supply relationships exist are the endogenous (i.e., jointly determined) variables. The remaining Q_i^j and the X_i^j are the exogenous (i.e., externally specified) variables of the model. As a simple example, suppose that on the demand side, the probability y of preferring mode 1 to mode 2 is a function of m = 2 attributes (Total Travel Time and Comfort) expressed as their relative attribute satisfaction ratings $Q_1 = Q_1^1 - Q_1^2$ and $Q_2 = Q_2^1 - Q_2^2$. On the supply side for mode 1 (Auto), Q_1^1 (Travel Time) is a function of the exogenous variables Q_3^1 (Traffic) and X_4^1 (Distance); and on the supply side for mode 2 (Transit), Q_1^2 (Travel Time) is a function of the exogenous variables Q_5^2 (Total Riding Time) and X_6^2 (Time between Departures). The auto comfort variable Q_2^1 is a function of traffic Q_3^1 and travel time Q_1^1 and transit comfort is exogenous.

The model may then be written as

$$y = a_0 + a_1 Q_1 + a_2 Q_2$$
$$Q_1 = Q_1^1 - Q_1^2$$
$$Q_2 = Q_2^1 - Q_2^2$$

$$Q_1^1 = c_{01}^1 + c_{11}^1 Q_3^1 + c_{21}^1 X_4^1$$

$$Q_1^2 = c_{01}^2 + c_{11}^2 Q_5^2 + c_{21}^2 X_6^2$$

$$Q_2^1 = c_{02}^1 + c_{12}^1 Q_3^1 + c_{22}^1 Q_1^1$$

where the variables Q_1^2, Q_1^1, Q_1, Q_2^1, Q_2 and y are the jointly determined endogenous variables of the model, and the remainder are considered exogenous. In order to obtain consistent estimates of importance, it is necessary to obtain estimates of the coefficients a_0, a_1, and a_2 via an appropriate simultaneous equation estimation procedure.

The important point to note is that even though the data used to estimate this model of consumer choice came from questioning consumers (the demand side), in general it is still necessary to introduce supply side relationships in order to obtain consistent estimates of the importance of product attributes. Since the nature of the supply side will vary from industry to industry, it is the objective of Part I. to focus on the demand side.

Another point which needs emphasis here is that this model has been developed in terms of perceived levels of attributes. If consumer perception differs widely from, say, engineering fact, it may be difficult to validate what are a priori realistic supply side relationships. In which case, there would appear to be no choice but to work with single equation demand models. This problem is discussed further below.

It should be mentioned that the estimated relative importances will depend on the pair of modes (or products) the traveller (or consumer) is asked to choose between. This arises, of course, from the fact that modal estimation and associated statistical inference require the assumption of fixed or non-stochastic values of the explanatory variables (i.e., relative attribute satisfaction values). If another pair of modes lead to significantly different relative attribute satisfaction ratings, then the model will need to be re-estimated. In most cases, the supply equations will change as well. In either case, re-estimation is required.

This need for re-estimation is not a retraction of the assumption that U_i and, therefore, M_i are independent of the mode (or product) under consideration. It is simply a result of the fact that a given mode pair may not provide sufficient variability of the attribute values X_i. However, it does seem likely that validity of the assumption of additive utilities would depend on the range of X_i as well. For these reasons, it is likely to be necessary to re-estimate these models using a number of different mode pairs if choice between a number of modes is of interest.

8. The Adequacy of an Attribute Description

A major question to be answered before proceeding to develop and estimate a simultaneous equation importance estimation model is whether or not it will be possible to predict consumer choice based on estimated importances and relative attribute satisfaction ratings. The issue being specifically addressed here is whether or not the set of (fifteen) attributes fully (or at least adequately) describe the alternative modes from a consumer point of view. Note that the relative importance of specific attributes is not at issue here. The argument being that if the set of relative attribute satisfaction ratings do not allow the prediction of mode choice with some degree of success, there would seem to be little sense in attempting to explain behavior based on the data. For this reason, it is desirable to perform a discriminant analysis.[30] The discriminant analysis results are given below.

In all cases, group 1 refers to the sample choosing automobile in preference to transit and group 2 refers to the sample choosing transit. The notation used in the tables below may be summarized as follows:

n_1	group 1 sample size
n_2	group 2 sample size
$n=n_1+n_2$	total sample size
$K=\log_e(n_2/n_1)$	classification rule criterion
$p_1=n_1/n$	a priori probability of classification in group 1
$p_2=n_2/n$	a priori probability of classification in group 2
$P_0=(p_1)^2+(p_2)^2$	"chance" probability of correct classification
$P=m/n$	proportion of sample correctly classified by discriminant-classification rule
$z=(P-P_0)/\sqrt{(P_0(1-P_0)/n}$	statistic to test significance of difference in proportions $(P-P_0)$
D^2	Mahalanobis sample distance statistic

[30] T. W. Anderson, An Introduction to Multivariate Statistical Analysis (John Wiley & Sons, Inc., New York, 1958).

In interpreting the results of Table III, it should be borne in mind that P is the proportion of individuals correctly classified within the sample by the sample discriminant-classification rule, and is consequently an upwardly biased estimate of the population correct classification rate.[31] Comparison of P_0 and P, therefore, gives an overly optimistic view of the predictive power. However, P appears to be much better than the chance probability P_0, and the statistical test of z against the critical z-value confirms that the difference is statistically significant at better than the 0.01% level. The D^2 statistic also confirms a highly significant difference in the sample means.

TABLE III

DISCRIMINANT-CLASSIFICATION ANALYSIS RESULTS

Choice made between auto mode and:	n_1	n_2	n	K	p_1	p_2	P_0	P	z	D^2
Rail transit	60	57	117	0.051	.513	.487	.500	.812	6.25	84.18

Critical z(0.01%) = +3.72

In order to resolve the question of the extent of the bias in the estimates of the correct classification rates P, a "jackknife" estimation method was used. The method is similar to that of Lachenbruch,[32] but in order to reduce the computation involved, the estimates were based on ten different discriminant functions per sample rather than the n suggested by Lachenbruch.

[31] For illustration of this bias see Ronald E. Frank, William F. Massy and Donald G. Morrison, "Bias in Multiple Discriminant Analysis," Journal of Marketing Research, Vol. 2 (August, 1965), pp. 255-258; and Olive Jean Dunn and Paul D. Varady, "Probabilities of Correct Classification in Discriminant Analysis," Biometrics, Vol. 22, Pt. 4 (1966), pp. 908-924.

[32] Peter A. Lachenbruch, "An Almost Unbiased Method of Obtaining Confidence Intervals for the Probability of Misclassification in Discriminant Analysis," Biometrics, Vol. 23, Pt. 4 (1967), pp. 639-645.

The resulting approximately unbiased estimates of correct classification rates, P', are compared to the corresponding biased estimates P in Table IV. Also given in Table IV are the "chance" probabilities P_0 and P'_0 which give the appropriate comparisons for P and P' respectively; the z-values to test the differences between P and P_0, and P' and P'_0; and the difference P - P' expressed as a fraction of P. The "chance" probabilities P_0 and P'_0 are different as a result of the slightly smaller sample sizes used in the "jackknife" estimates.

TABLE IV

COMPARISON OF BIASED AND APPROXIMATELY UNBIASED CORRECT CLASSIFICATION RATES

Sample	Biased Estimates				Approximately Unbiased Estimates				
	n	P	P_0	z	n	P'	P'_0	z	$\frac{P-P'}{P}$
Auto/rail transit	117	.812	.500	6.25	110	.736	.505	4.85	.094

Critical z(0.01%) = 3.72

The results indicate that there is an appreciable upward bias in the correct classification estimates P, but the unbiased estimate P' is still very highly significantly different from the "chance" correct classification rate. The conclusion that there is significant discriminatory power in the data, thus, is not changed by a knowledge of the bias in P. Moreover, since the analysis was in terms of relative attribute satisfaction ratings (i.e., difference), these results support the view that the semantic differential technique provided interval scaled data - a requirement of the demand model.

Interpretation of the constant term in the demand equation can assist in determining the nature of omitted attributes in the linear model

$$y = a_0 + \sum_i a_i Q_i$$

where y is the probability of preferring auto, the constant term a_0 indicates the probability that the typical individual will prefer auto to transit if all the Q_i are zero, i.e., if his satisfactions with the two modes are equal for all attributes.

For the sample under study, the a priori probability of preferring auto was 60/117 = 0.513. The estimated value of a_0 was 0.477. The null hypothesis $a_0 = .513$ cannot be rejected even at the 50 percent level. Based on these findings and those of the discriminant analysis it would appear that the original set of 15 attributes provide an adequate description of the two modes in question from a consumer choice point of view.

In Table V are given the sample discriminant function coefficients associated with the attributes i = 1,...,15. It is important to note that these weights have often been referred to as relative importances in the literature.[33] As discussed in Section 6, these weights are not consistent estimates of importances as defined in Section 5. It is true that in the two group case, discriminant analysis weights will be proportional to those of a regression analysis with a dummy dependent variable implying that the linear demand equation (4.19) developed in Section 4 could be estimated in either way. Note, however, that there is no classical linear regression model equivalent to discriminant analysis for more than two groups, and that only the regression model permits statistical inference regarding the relative importance of attributes. Statistical inference using discriminant analysis must be confined to the statistical significance of a particular set of attributes in predicting group membership not the individual relative importance of the attributes.

---

[33] Green and Tull, p. 370 and Myers and Alpert, p. 18

TABLE V

DISCRIMINANT FUNCTION COEFFICIENTS

Attributes[a]

1	2	3	4	5	6	7	8	9	10	11	12	13	14	15
-0.06	0.36	0.02	0.03	0.22	-0.26	-0.10	0.18	-0.03	-0.09	0.12	0.05	0.17	0.51	0.25

a the attributes are defined in Table I

9. Reduction of Semantic Redundancy

Developing a set of attributes that fully describes a group of products from a consumer point of view is a tedious process. A list of potential attributes and their end points must be developed with meanings clear to the respondent. In general, it is not possible to develop a list which does not contain some semantic redundancy. Usually the initial list will become quite long. One of the authors used 65 different semantic differentials to describe automobiles in a product clinic designed to pretest Chevrolet's Vega.

Table I showed a list of the 15 attributes for which satisfaction ratings were obtained. It is clear the fifteen attributes may contain semantic redundancy. An equal-tails test of the null hypothesis that the true population correlation coefficient for any pair of variables is zero gives critical points of 0.182 at the 5% level and 0.238 at the 1% level. Examination of the correlation matrix indicated that of the 205 elements to one side of the principal diagonal, 67 were greater than 0.238, demonstrating that, statistically speaking, many highly significant correlations existed.

These high intercorrelations give rise to the problem of multicollinearity if these correlated attributes are included as explanatory variables in a multiple regression model. The problem of multicollinearity in regression analysis is a perplexing one arising frequently in econometric studies; it is discussed, for example, by Goldberger.[34] The problem arises in interpreting the estimated coefficients of the regression since, if high intercorrelations exist between some, or all, of the explanatory variables, it becomes difficult if not impossible to distinguish between the separate influences of the explanatory variables and obtain a reasonably precise estimate of their relative importances. Multicollinearity has the effect of producing large standard errors of the coefficients for the explanatory variables of an equation; as intercorrelations become higher, confidence in the reliability of the coefficient estimates is reduced.[35]

Because of this problem and the additive utility assumption, it is desirable to reduce the original set of attributes to a smaller set by removing those attributes that are highly correlated to others due to semantic problems. It is important to point out here that care must be taken from the outset to identify those correlations which are likely to be due to supply side relationships and those that are due to semantic problems. This is accomplished most simply by establishing on an a priori basis those attributes which are likely to be correlated for supply side reasons, e.g., auto out-of-pocket cost and traffic. The objective here is to suggest a technique for handling the problems caused by semantic redundancies which also assists in developing a nearly orthogonal set of attributes.

It seems plausable to suppose that the traveller thinks in terms of a smaller number of (orthogonal) decision "factors" rather than the fifteen attributes given in the questionnaire. In fact, the demand model is constructed on the basis of additive utilities. But several attributes, for example, "comfort" and "pleasantness" may actually be closely related to the same dimension of the mode choice process because the words "comfort" and "pleasantness" may mean about the same

[34-35] Goldberger, pp. 192-194.

thing to people when applied to a mode of transportation.

This hypothesis is supported by a correlation of 0.7 between, for example, attributes 1 (comfort) and 5 (pleasantness). Hence, it seems likely that several attributes are closely related to essentially the same dimension of the modal choice decision. The problem arising out of this hypothesis -- that of analyzing the basic dimensionality of a sample of observations on a large number of variables -- can be addressed by factor analysis.[36]

A principal components type factor analysis on all 15 relative attribute satisfaction ratings (Q_i) was performed. Varimax rotation of the first nine principal components was also performed as an aid to interpretation. The results are summarized in Table VI.

[36] H. H. Harman, Modern Factor Analysis (University of Chicago Press, Chicago, 1967), p. 4.

TABLE VI

SUMMARY OF VARIMAX ROTATED FACTOR MATRIX[a]

Rail Transit Sample (Rotation of First Nine Components)

Percent of Variance Explained = 88%

Rotated Factor	Attributes within factor with absolute factor loadings > 0.30				Factor Interpretation
1	6 (.90)	1 (.87)	7 (.74)	5 (.68)	physical comfort
	11 (.62)	13 (.33)	9 (.33)		
2	8 (.87)	5 (.38)	10 (.38)		congestion
3	4 (.90)	15 (.60)	11 (.40)		service frequency
4	14 (.98)				walking time
5	3 (.93)				weather exposure
6	2 (-.81)	15 (-.45)	13 (-.40)		dependability
7	9 (.87)	11 (.38)			social comfort
8	10 (.83)	13 (.53)			riding time
9	12 (-.85)	13 (-.52)			cost

[a] See Table I for attribute definitions

Nine of the possible 15 principal components are listed in Table VI. The choice of the nine factors can be justified by the fact that the 88% of variance explained is substantial, but equally importantly these nine may be interpreted as modal choice "decision factors" in a way which is intuitively satisfying. Attributes, 6 (vehicle attractiveness), 5 (pleasantness), 1 (comfort), and 7 (noise) are the attributes with the highest loading in factor 1; 10 (traffic) and 8 (accidents) have the highest loading in factor 2; 4 (frequency) and 15 (waiting time) have the highest loading in factor 3. Conversely, attribute 14 (walking time) is the only variable with a high loading in factor 4, and this is consistent with the "prior" that walking time is relatively independent of other mode attributes. It was difficult to interpret the factors beyond the ninth as "different" dimensions of the modal choice decision. It is interesting to note that Green and Rao have suggested that at least eight attributes be used to describe a product.[37]

In general, the principal components analysis of a set of variables which are prospective regressors in a multiple regression equation may be used in alleviating the multicollinearity problem in two ways. Firstly, the principal components solution may be used directly as suggested, for example, by Kloek and Mennes.[38] The m-element vector of observations on the original variables is replaced by the p-element vector of linear combinations of the variable (i.e., factor "scores") which are obtained by multiplication of the original variables by the loadings given in the principal components factor matrix. These p factor scores are then used as the explanatory variables of the regression.

[37] Green and Rao, p. 38.

[38] T. Kloek and L. E. M. Mennes, "Simultaneous Estimation Based on Principal Components of Predetermined Variables," Econometrica, Vol. 28 (January, 1960), pp. 45-61.

Obviously, however, the regression coefficient estimates will not be the same for the two regressions. In fact, the difficulties involved in interpreting the coefficients of the factor score regression represent the major drawback of the use of this method in structural analysis. The interpretation of a regression coefficient as the magnitude of the effect on the dependent variable produced by a unit change in an explanatory variable (factor) becomes difficult where the explanatory variable is a linear combination of the observed variables (relative attribute satisfaction ratings). Very often the sum of the weights for those attributes not loading heavily is higher than the sum of the larger weights which provided the factor interpretation. Moreover, the absence of well-tried means of testing the statistical significance of the coefficients estimated via principal components analysis further complicates interpretation of the regression coefficients. Thus, while the method of using the principal components solution directly in the multiple regression does remove the multicollinearity problem and is considered by some to introduce a certain objectivity to the estimation procedure, it is of little help where the aim is interpretation of the coefficients of the regression equation as structural parameters.

An alternative use of the principal components analysis in reducing the effects of multicollinearity is to select a subset of p from the m original variable on the basis of their factor loadings in the p principal components (which account for "most" of the sample variance) and perform the regression on this subset of the original variables. The most obvious criterion is to select those p variables which have the highest loadings in each of the p components. The resulting set of variables will tend to have low intercorrelations, thus reducing (although not eliminating) multicollinearity, and importantly, the use of the actually observed variable in the regression simplifies interpretation of the associated coefficients. Furthermore, the method allows the inclusion or exclusion of any of the variables dictated by supply side considerations on grounds of the model structure.

Use of principal components analysis in this latter indirect way would then seem to be a much more appropriate method than the former in most instances where regression coefficients are to be interpreted structurally. It should be remarked that selection of a subset of the original variables so that highly intercorrelated variables are omitted is the standard procedure for dealing with multicollinearity in regression; the use of principal components analysis in the way outlined here merely provides a systematic and rational basis for selection of the variable to be included. This view is supported by Green and Tull in their review of the usefullness of principal components analysis.[39]

In this case, the principal components analysis of relative attribute satisfaction data indicates that fewer than 15 attributes adequately account for the dimensionality of the modal choice decision; the first nine factors are intuitively interpretable as "different" dimensions. These nine are, moreover, fairly easily identified with attributes in the original list of fifteen so that the method discussed above is helpful in selecting variables for subsequent regression analysis. Accordingly, on the basis of the principal components analysis, the following nine attributes were selected for further analysis:

1	Comfort in vehicle
2	Dependability of on time arrival
3	Protection from weather while waiting
9	Exposure to undesirable behavior of others
10	Traffic
12	Out-of-pocket cost
13	Total time spent riding
14	Total time spent walking
15	Total time spent waiting

Although many of the correlations among these nine were still statis-

---

[39]Green and Tull, pp. 422-426.

tically significant, the very high correlations present in the fifteen variable set of attributes were removed. The multicollinearity problem is, thus, still present, but its seriousness is lessened. Strictly speaking, it is now necessary to be sure that the reduced set of attributes is adequate, that is, repeat the discriminant analysis procedure.

Although it is assumed the retained attributes form a set which, in fact, represent the various dimensions of the modal choice as perceived by the traveller, there may still remain correlations among the relative attribute satisfaction ratings due to supply relationships. For example, examination of the correlations for the nine attributes listed above revealed that the highest correlations occurred between attributes 12 (cost) and 13 (riding time), 10 (traffic) and 13 (riding time), and 2 (dependability) and 15 (waiting time). These correlations do not, however, arise for "semantic" reasons but for reasons which may be labelled "supply side oriented;" that is, cost and riding time are correlated because there is a functional dependency between cost and riding time, not because travellers understand the same thing by "out-of-pocket cost" and "total time spent riding." In this sense, the correlations between traffic and riding time, and dependability and waiting time also arise as a result of such supply side relationships (although the correlation matrix obviously does not indicate the direction of causality of the relationships).

Note also that the "semantic" correlations are traveller-dependent and, hence, arise from relationships on what have been termed the demand side while the "functional" correlations arise from relationships which are logically mode-dependent and arise on the supply side. In other words, it is up to the analyst to determine the relevant supply side relationships and provide the linkage between supply and demand.

Thus, correlations among these data arise for both "semantic" and supply side reasons. It is important to appreciate that while principal components analysis is helpful in summarizing the data in a way which facilitates recognition of the former, it is of little help in distinguishing between the two. The analysis method is, in other words, unable to identify the underlying causalties which define the structure of the data. It is important to note that the factor analysis has been done in terms of relative attribute satisfaction ratings rather than separately for each mode -- auto and transit. Since the modes have different supply side relationships, using relative attribute satisfaction ratings tends to confound the supply sides leaving the semantic problems. Separate principal components analysis for each mode lead to results which did not yield to logical interpretation even with varimax rotation.

It should be noted that in this case, the principal components analysis support the view that the "experiment" underlying the attribute satisfaction and modal choice data is not a simple "single equation" economic process but a complex process of interrelated and simultaneous relationships. The modal choice decision "experiment" generates observations which reflect the equilibrium of supply and demand relationships; a properly structured model of modal choice must then make explicit the simultaneous interaction of these supply and demand relationships.

10. The Validation of Some Crucial Assumptions

The object of this section is to validate some of the important assumptions of the demand equation formulation given in Section 4. Recall that for comfort-type attributes, the assumed relationship for the exponential type utility function and linear U to Q mapping is

10.1) $$Q_i^j = 1+(k-1)(1-e^{-\lambda_i x_i^j})$$

and for cost-type attributes, the assumed relationship is

10.2) $$Q_i^j = 1 + (k-1)\, e^{-\lambda_i X_i^j}$$

where k is the number of intervals on the semantic scale, equal to 7 for this data. An alternative relationship between Q_i^j and X_i^j can be developed on the basis of a linear utility function and the linear U to Q mapping. It has the linear form

10.3) $$Q_i^j = \mu_{0i} + \mu_i X_i^j$$

where the parameter μ_i is positive for comfort-type attributes and negative for cost-type attributes.

It will be remembered that relationships (10.1) and (10.2) are central to the construction of the demand equation of the model and the linear U to Q mapping assumption leads to the interpretation of the parameters of that equation as "importances." It is desirable then to investigate the validity of both the exponential relationships of equations (10.1) and (10.2) and the linear equation (10.3) inasfar as the data allow.

In the data a sample of observations are given on both Q_i^j and the corresponding X_i^j for the following attributes.

Attribute Satisfaction Rating	Attribute Value
Automobile Mode	
Total time spent riding (QA13)	Total riding time (minutes) (XA13)
Total time spent walking (QA14)	Total walking time (minutes) (XA14)
Transit Mode	
Frequency of vehicle departure times (QT4)	Headway of vehicle departures (minutes) (XT4)
Out-of-pocket cost (QT12)	Fare (XT18)
Total time spent riding (QT13)	Total riding time (XT13)
Total time spent walking (QT14)	Total walking time (XT14)
Total time spent waiting (QT15)	Total waiting time (XT15)

From the sample of 117 individuals making a choice between automobile and rail transit a subsample of 84 gave complete responses on all variables listed above. This subsample is used to estimate the assumed Q/X relationships in this section. The estimations of both the exponential and linear forms are given below.

All the attributes listed above are what have been termed cost-type attributes, i.e., increasing values of the attribute are associated with decreasing utility levels. This is the case simply because attribute value measurements are not available for the comfort-type attributes which tend to be qualitative attributes. Therefore, only the relationships of the form of equations (10.2) and (10.3) can be estimated.

Rewriting equation (10.2) as a regression equation

10.4) $$(Q_i^j - 1) = K_i e^{-\lambda_i X_i^j}$$

where $\mathcal{K}_i$ and λ_i are both parameters to be estimated. It is necessary to estimate equation (10.4) directly by nonlinear regression in order to obtain estimates of $\mathcal{K}_i$ and λ_i. The results given in Table VIII below were estimated by a nonlinear least squares algorithm described by Hartley.[40] Before studying these results, the following points should be made.

From comparison of equations (10.2) and 10.4), it would be expected that the estimated value of $\mathcal{K}_i$ would be equal to (k-1) or 6 that is, independent of the attribute i if the hypothesized relationship between Q_i^j and X_i^j fit the data exactly. The closeness of the coefficient $\mathcal{K}_i$ to 6 in results given below is, therefore, an indication of the validity of the relationship and, hence, the assumption of an exponential utility function and linear U to Q mapping.

The R^2 statistics given for the regression results are computed from one minus the ratio of the sum of squares about the exponential regression curve (the sum of squared residuals) to the sum of squares about the mean. This indicates the goodness of fit to the data of a regression curve of the form shown in figure 10.1.

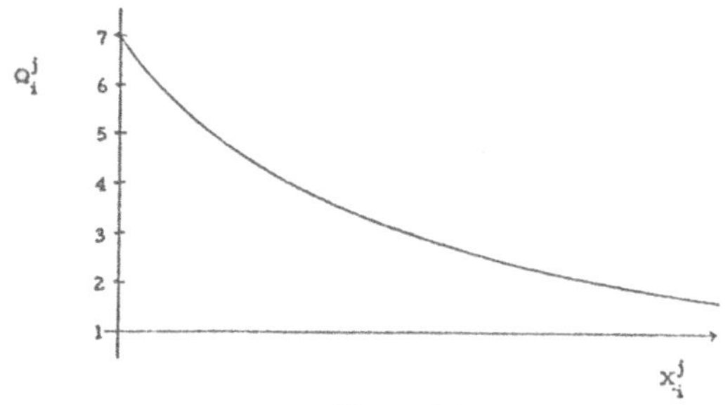

fig. 10.1

However, the observations on Q_i^j being fitted are not continuous over the interval 1 to 7, as figure 10.1 implies, but integer valued. This

[40] Hartley, pp. 269-280

being the case, the appropriate curve by which to judge fit should really be a step-function as shown in figure 10.2.

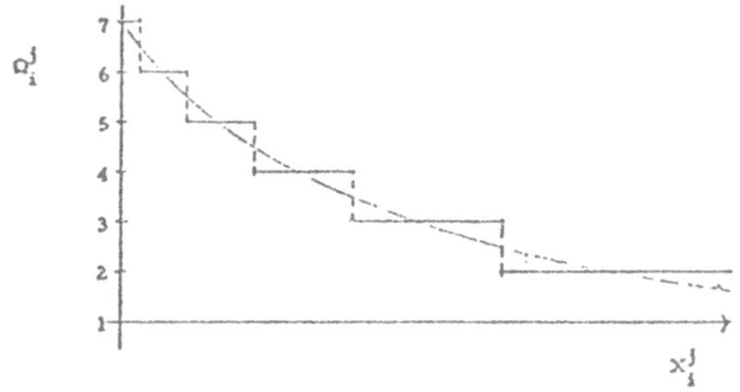

If all observed points fell on the step function, it would be as good a fit as possible; the sum of squared residuals about the exponential regression curve would, however, obviously not be zero, and hence, the R^2 statistic would be less than one. In general, the sum of squares about the regression curve tends to be greater than that about the step function, and consequently the R^2 statistics tabulated below tend to give conservative indications of the goodness of fit. As a supplemental measure of the fit of the data to the regression curve, for each equation, the proportion of observations on Q_i^j having values within $\pm$ 1 of the predicted value was computed and is given in Table VII as "Proportion Fitted $\pm$ 1." The t-statistics given for the estimates of K are the appropriate statistics to test the null hypothesis the $\hat{K} = 6$. The t-statistics computed for the λ estimates are the familiar null t-statistics.

The results of Table VII show a convincing fit of the exponential Q/X relationship to the data for the six attributes included. The estimated values for K are all close to 6, and the associated t-statistics show that statistically speaking (with one exception), the differences from 6 are insignificant (judging significance under the usual assumptions of normality) for all estimates. The t-statistics associated with λ estimates also indicate these all to be reliable. The R^2

statistics, although not very large, are in all cases highly significant and indicate reasonably close fits -- given the nature of the data. For example, no stratification based on demographics has been made. The proportions of fitted values within ± 1 of the observed values also indicate reasonable fits.

TABLE VII

SUMMARY OF ESTIMATED EXPONENTIAL Q/X RELATIONSHIPS

$(Q - 1) = Ke^{-\lambda X}$ Sample Size = 84

Attribute	Variable Q	Variable X	Estimated[a] K	Estimated[b] λ	Regression R^2	Proportion[c] Fitted ±1
Automobile Riding Time	QA13	XA13	7.09 (1.49)	.0199 (5.48)	.353	.667
Automobile Walking Time	QA14	XA14	6.08 (0.34)	.0253 (3.71)	.153	.881
Transit Frequency	QT4	XT4	5.28 (-2.26)	.0172 (3.55)	.178	.667
Transit Riding Time	QT13	XT13	5.59 (-0.73)	.0148 (3.91)	.192	.512
Transit Walking Time	QT14	XT14	5.79 (-0.44)	.0245 (3.61)	.153	.643
Transit Waiting Time	QT15	XT15	5.97 (-0.09)	.0416 (5.88)	.425	.798

Critical t (5%) = 1.989   Critical t (1%) = 2.637   Critical R^2 (1%) = 0.078

[a] t-statistic in parentheses to test null hypothesis $K = 6$

[b] t-statistic in parentheses to test null hypothesis $\lambda = 0$

[c] explanation given in text

The regression of equation (10.4) was also performed on the data with the constant term K constrained to equal 6, in order to give estimates for the parameter λ which could be compared between attributes. These results are given in Table VIII.

TABLE VIII

SUMMARY OF ESTIMATED EXPONENTIAL Q/X RELATIONSHIPS

$(Q - 1) = 6\,e^{-\lambda X}$ Sample Size = 84

Attribute	Variable Q	Variable X	Estimated λ	Regression R^2
Automobile Riding Time	QA13	XA13	.0150	.332
Automobile Walking Time	QA14	XA14	.0235	.152
Transit Frequency	QT4	XT4	.0258	.128
Transit Riding Time	QT13	XT13	.0171	.186
Transit Walking Time	QT14	XT14	.0271	.151
Transit Waiting Time	QT15	XT15	.0422	.425

Critical R^2 (1%) = 0.078

Interesting results from Table VIII are the values of the parameter estimates for the attributes riding time and walking time for the automobile and transit modes, viz:

	Auto	Transit
Riding Time	.015	.017
Walking Time	.024	.027

Note the closeness of the λ values for riding time and for walking time. Recall that in the demand model formulation it was assumed that the satisfaction or utility obtained from a given modal attribute level is independent of the mode considered. The closeness of the above λ estimates provides an interesting validation of this assumption.

The results given in Table IX are for the estimations of equation (10.3) which may be estimated via the linear regression equation

$$Q_i^j = \mu_{0i} + \mu_i X_i^j$$

where

where μ_0 and μ_i are parameters to be estimated. Note that for cost-type attributes, the regression results are for the same sample of 84 observations as were used in the nonlinear estimations. The R^2 statistics are all significant and although not high, are close to those given for the corresponding exponential relationships in Table VIII, indicating a similar fit to the data. The t-statisitcs on μ also indicate all estimated coefficients to be significantly greater than zero at a 1% confidence level. Note that as expected for cost-type attributes a μ_0 of approximately seven was obtained. The null hypothesis $\mu_0 = 7$ is not rejected at the 1% level in all cases but one.

Two important assumptions of the model have been supported by the evidence provided here. The first was that the U_i could be specified to be mode independent. The second assumption was that of a linear mapping from U to Q. This assumption is critical to the determination of importance via estimates of a_i. The assumption appears to stand up well in connection with either an exponential or linear utility function assumption. The final basic assumption used in deriving the demand relationship viz. additive utilities implies that need to specify an attribute description which is (nearly) orthogonal from a semantic point of view. Methods for accomplishing this were discussed in Section 7. Note that correlation due to supply side relationships do not cause difficulties in this regard.

TABLE IX

SUMMARY OF ESTIMATED LINEAR Q/X RELATIONSHIPS

$Q = \mu_0 - \mu X$ Sample Size = 84

Attribute	Variable Q	Variable X	Estimated[b] μ_0	Estimated[a] μ	Regression R^2
Automobile Riding Time	QA13	XA13	6.98 (-0.05)	.0641 (6.68)	.352
Automobile Walking Time	QA14	XA14	7.04 (0.19)	.1319 (3.84)	.152
Transit Frequency	QT4	XT4	6.21 (-3.09)	.0722 (4.45)	.194
Transit Riding Time	QT13	XT13	6.42 (-1.43)	.0587 (4.71)	.213
Transit Walking Time	QT14	XT14	6.67 (-0.86)	.1087 (3.95)	.160
Transit Waiting Time	QT15	XT15	6.57 (-2.03)	.1455 (8.02)	.440

Critical t (5%) = 1.989 Critical t (1%) = 2.637 Critical R^2 = 0.078

[a]t-statistic in parentheses is to test the null hypothesis $\mu = 0$

[b]" " " " " " " " " " $\mu_0 = 7$

11. Estimation of the Utility Function Parameters of Target Markets

One of the areas requiring additional research is that of estimating utility functions of various consumer groups -- so called target markets. The results reported here are preliminary but encouraging. Assume a demand function of the form of equation (4.19). Note that in order to estimate relative importances M_i/M_m as a function of demographics, it is only necessary to stratify the sample into different groups and perform an independent analysis for each group. This was not possible here due to degree of freedom problems given the sample size available.

However, an attempt was made to estimate the Q/X relationship as a function of income. While, perhaps, not obvious it turns out that it is difficult to develop unassailable hypotheses as to how changes in income will affect the λ parameter of the utility function. Only waiting time appears straightforward. The higher income, the larger the expected $|\lambda|$. The following model was estimated via nonlinear estimation

$$Q_i - 1 = 6e^{-\lambda x_i}$$

where $\lambda = A + BY + CY^2$ with A, B and C as parameters and Y as a dummy income variable. The adjusted R^2 was .45 compared to .43 for the λ = constant model (Table VIII) where the λ estimate was - .0422. The table below shows $-\lambda$ as a function of income.

Income Group	$\lvert\lambda\rvert$ Value
5,000 - 7,000	.0218
7,000 - 10,000	.0378
10,000 - 15,000	.0460
Over 15,000	.0461

As expected $\lvert\lambda\rvert$ increases with income indicating that dissatisfaction over waiting time increases with income.

12. Estimates of Relative Importance and Model Structure

The purpose of this section is to show that estimates of the parameters of the demand equation and, therefore, estimates of importances are highly sensitive to model structure. These estimates are not only sensitive to demand side structure, but also very sensitive to the insertion of a supply side into the model. Three different models will be considered.

Model 1 is the single equation linear probability model given by equation (4.19). Estimation was by ordinary least squares. Recall that parameter estimates are inefficient, that is, not minimum variance due to the heteroskedasticity problem. Also recall that model structure is poor since the function is illogical at the ends. Of course, ignoring the supply side implies that the estimates are not only inefficient, but also inconsistent. Given that this model and discriminant analysis yield identical estimates of "relative importances," this is probably the most frequently applied statistical inference model for determining attribute importances.

Model 2 is also a single equation importance estimation model, the logistic function demand model is given by equation (4.21). This model was estimated via nonlinear least squares. The estimation procedure would yield the best unbiased estimates if the data used to calibrate the model were not the result of supply and demand interaction. Hence, the estimates are inconsistent.

Model 3 is a simultaneous equation model incorporating the supply side developed by Sherret.[41] The model has the general form given by equations (7.1), (7.2) and (7.3). Five supply equations were developed. Since the model utilizes the linear probability demand function, parameter estimates are still inefficient. However, the estimation procedure used, essentially two stage least squares, yields consistent estimates of the parameters. Hence, model 3 parameter estimates are consistent but inefficient.

Table X shows the estimates of relative importance obtained via each of the three models. For comparison purposes four attributes are shown: walking time, dependability, waiting time and riding time. The first important point to note is that the two single equation models (1 and 2) yield very different results. Both yield one parameter estimate which is insignificant. In fact, waiting time and riding time reverse roles in the two models, one of the two being insignificant and, therefore, least important in both models. Note that both models 1 and 2 imply that walking time is most important and dependability is next most important. In terms of the t-statistic, model 2 does provide lower variance estimates.

---

[41]Sherret, "Structuring an Econometric Model of Mode Choice."

TABLE X

COMPARISON OF IMPORTANCE ESTIMATION MODELS

	MODEL 1			MODEL 2			MODEL 3		
ATRRIBUTE	Estimated Coefficient	t-statistic	Relative Importance	Estimated Coefficient	t-statistic	Relative Importance	Estimated Coefficient	t-statistic	Relative Importance
Q14 (Walking Time)	0.0706	3.569	1.000	0.6091	3.589	1.000	0.0804	4.232	1.000
Q2 (Dependability)	0.0525	2.712	0.744	0.4333	2.802	0.711	0.1027	2.936	1.277
Q15 (Waiting Time)	0.0447	2.063	0.633	0.2283	1.547	0.375	0.0493	2.110	0.613
Q13 (Riding Time)	0.0233	1.139	0.330	0.3577	2.286	0.587	0.0647	2.903	0.804

Critical $t_{0.025,111} = 1.981$

Model 3 yields estimates of relative importance which are very different from either model 1 or model 2. All of the parameter estimates are significant, in fact, for all four attributes the t-statistic is highest for model 3. Moreover, dependability is found to be most important, with walking time second, riding time third and waiting time least important. The rank order importances for the three models are shown below.

	Model 1	Model 2	Model 3
Dependability	2	2	1
Walking Time	1	1	2
Riding Time	4	3	3
Waiting Time	3	4	4

While the results of model 3 seem most sensible to the authors, the point is that they are very much different than those of the other two models. It seems that supply side considerations simply cannot be ignored.

As an aside, it should be mentioned here that in practice it would be wise to also obtain measures of importance directly from consumers in addition to the statistical inference technique suggested above.

This can be done via the semantic differential with end points "very important" to "very unimportant."[42] Paine et al measured attribute satisfaction ratings and importances for the mode choice decision problem via the semantic differential.[43] It is interesting to note that their results regarding relative importance were similar to those obtained above in that "reliability of destination achievement" was found to be most important with "travel time" second where travel time included expected value of travel time and dependability of on time arrival. They also found comfort-type attributes way down the list in terms of importance for the work trip mode choice. Paine et al, however, determine only rank order importances and make no attempt to relate their results to the choices people actually make.

13. An Application of the Results

The purpose of this section is to illustrate how the estimated importances can be used along with the attribute satisfaction data in advertising and/or product planning. Table XI shows mean relative attribute satisfaction ratings broken down by first choice auto and transit. Note that as expected both groups give auto the edge for walking and waiting time but disagree concerning dependability of on time arrival and riding time.

---

[42] Mark I. Alpert, "Identification of Determinant Attributes: A Comparison of Methods," Journal of Marketing Research, Vol. VIII (May, 1971), pp. 184-190.

[43] Frank T. Paine, Allan N. Nash, Stanley J. Hille and Allen G. Brunner "Consumer Attitudes toward Auto versus Public Transport Alternatives," Journal of Applied Psychology, Vol. 53, No. 6 (1969), p. 474.

TABLE XI

RELATIVE ATTRIBUTE SATISFACTION RATINGS

(Auto - Transit)

Attribute	Mean First Choice Auto	Mean First Choice Transit
Dependability	.67	- 1.70
Walking Time	1.73	0.42
Riding Time	0.78	- 1.08
Waiting Time	1.97	0.25

Table XII shows mean attribute satisfaction ratings for auto and transit separately by first choice auto and transit. Assume the question of interest is how to improve patronage of transit via advertising.

TABLE XII

ATTRIBUTE SATISFACTION RATINGS

	Automobile Ratings		Rail Transit Ratings		
Attribute	Mean First Choice Auto	Mean First Choice Transit	Mean First Choice Auto	Mean First Choice Transit	DIFF
Dependability	5.42	4.23	4.75	5.95	1.20
Walking Time	6.52	6.53	4.78	6.10	1.32
Riding Time	5.05	4.45	4.27	5.54	1.27
Waiting Time	6.67	6.35	4.70	6.10	1.31

The DIFF column shows the difference between mean ratings of transit given by those choosing transit and those choosing auto. Along with auto ratings, it provides some information for estimating $\Delta Q/\Delta C$, that is, the degree to which it may be possible to change the transit ratings of people who chose auto. Walking time may be ruled out immediately on the assumption that people know how far it is to the nearest transit stop. Given the attribute importances, the decision between advertising regarding dependability, riding time or waiting time (frequency of service) depends on the $\Delta Q/\Delta C$ estimates. These estimates could be obtained via pretesting ads with auto commuters. As discussed in Section 5, the product of relative importance $\Delta U/\Delta Q$ and

$\Delta Q/\Delta C$ is the test criterion. However, since dependability is twice as important as waiting time and 50% more important than riding time and it is likely that commuters are aware of the schedules, it would seem that dependability would get the nod.

From the point of view of product planning, rail transit patronage would seem to be severely hampered due to its fixed route nature and the associated walking time required. This suggests the possibility of developing multi-mode transportation systems. Such systems are currently under study.[44]

14. Summary and Conclusions

The object of this work was to outline and illustrate a methodology for estimating the relative importance of product attributes. Product attribute descriptions were developed in terms of attribute satisfaction ratings obtained via a particular type of semantic differential. This was required due to the qualitative nature of many attributes. Satisfaction ratings, rather than attribute ratings, were obtained due to the apparently insurmountable difficulties in obtaining reliable measures of the latter for qualitative attributes.

The use of attribute satisfaction ratings rather than attribute ratings required the development of a family of demand relationships specified in terms of attribute satisfaction ratings. It was shown that relative importances could be defined in the context of the parameters of these relationships.

In a choice between two products, the probability of preferring product 1 to product 2 was determined to depend on the consumer's satisfaction with both products on each product attribute (relative

---

[44] E. T. Canty, James P. Wallace III, et al, New Systems Implementation Study, Research Publication GMR-710B (Prepared for HUD, General Motors Research Laboratories, Warren, Michigan, February, 1968).

attribute satisfaction ratings) and the relative importance of each of these product attributes. Attribute importance was determined to be proportional to the maximum utility obtainable from any level of the attribute.

Next, it was argued that correlations between attribute satisfaction ratings were likely to arise for two reasons: The first is the existence of supply side relationships; the second is semantic redundancy in the set of attributes. Failure to explicitly specify these supply side relationships will lead to inconsistent estimates of importances. Failure to handle the semantic redundancy problem will lead to importance estimates with unduly high variance.

It was suggested that discriminant analysis and principal components-type factor analysis be used in an iterative fashion to develop a set of attributes that "fully" describe the product from a consumer point of view but are as orthogonal as possible.

The demand side relationships were developed on the basis of three fundamental assumptions: additive utilities, exponential utility function specified independent of the product and a linear mapping from utilities to attribute satisfaction ratings. Empirical evidence of the validity of the latter two assumptions was provided. Some evidence was provided that it may be possible to estimate relative importance as a function of demographic variables.

Next, it was shown that estimates of relative importances vary greatly depending on model specifications. It was argued that the most frequently used statistical inference model is likely to lead to importance estimates which are both inefficient and inconsistent. A methodology is suggested which can lead to estimates which are both efficient and consistent.

Finally, an attempt was made to illustrate how relative attribute satisfaction ratings and relative importances can actually be used to facilitate advertising and/or product planning.

In conclusion, it appears that while considerable time and money will be required to develop an importance estimation model based on the methodology described above, the payoff in terms of improved understanding of the consumer decision making process can be considerable. Part II is an illustration of the proposed methodology where particular emphasis is placed on structuring the supply side of an importance estimation model.

PART II. A Simultaneous Equation Model for Estimating Mode Attribute Importances

1. Introduction

Two fundamentally different methods have been used to determine the relative importance of mode attributes in the mode choice decision making process. The first, called the attitudinal approach, is simply to ask respondents via some sort of scaling procedure to rate the mode attributes as to their importance.[1]

---

[1]Frank T. Paine, Allan N. Nash, Stanley J. Hille and Allen G. Brunner, Consumer Conceived Attributes of Transportation: An Attitude Study (Department of Business Administration, University of Maryland, College Park, Maryland, June, 1967).

Frank T. Paine, Allan N. Nash, Stanley J. Hille and Allen G. Brunner, "Consumer Attitudes toward Auto versus Public Transport Alternatives," Journal of Applied Psychology, Vol. 53, No. 6 (1969), pp. 472-480.

Individual Preferences for Various Means of Transportation (Management Science Center, University of Pennsylvania, May, 1965).

Alexis N. Sommers, "Expanding Nondemographic Factors in Modal Split Models" (Paper presented to the 36th National Meeting of ORSA, Miami, Florida, November 12, 1969).

The second method, termed the inferential method, seeks to infer attribute importances from data on mode preference and mode attribute ratings.[2] It is generally argued that the latter procedure is to be preferred, in that respondents are considered to be unwilling or unable to give their "true" feelings relevant to attribute importance. Although there has been considerable discussion of the simultaneous equation nature of the mode choice decision making process,[3] there

---

[2]Charles A. Lave, "A Behavioral Approach to Modal Split Forecasting," Transportation Research, Vol. 3, No. 4 (1969), pp. 463-480.

T. E. Lisco, "The Value of Commuter's Travel Time: A Study in Urban Transportation" (Unpublished Ph.D. Dissertation, University of Chicago, 1967).

Richard E. Quandt and William J. Baumol, "The Demand for Abstract Transport Modes: Theory and Measurement," Journal of Regional Science, Vol. 6, No. 2 (1966).

Stanley L. Warner, Stochastic Choice of Mode in Urban Travel: A Study in Binary Choice (Northwestern University Press, Evanston, Illinois, 1962).

D. A. Quarmby, "Choice of Travel Mode for the Journey to Work: Some Findings," Journal of Transport Economics and Policy, Vol. 1, No. 3 (1967), pp. 273-314.

Peter R. Stopher, "Predicting Travel Mode Choice for the Work Journey," Traffic Engineering and Control, Vol. 9, No. 9 (1968), pp. 436-439.

Peter R. Stopher, "A Probability Model of Travel Mode Choice for the Work Journey," Highway Research Record No. 283 (Highway Research Board, Washington, D.C., 1969).

Robert G. McGillivray, "Demand and Choice Models of Modal Split," Journal of Transport Economics and Policy, Vol. 4, No. 2 (1970), pp. 192-207

[3]Martin Beckmann, C. B. McGuire and Christopher B. Winsten, Studies in the Economics of Transportation (Yale University Press, New Haven, Connecticut, 1956).

Martin Wohl and Brian V. Martin, Traffic Systems Analysis for Engineers and Planners (McGraw-Hill Book Company, New York, 1967).

Gerald Kraft and Martin Wohl, "New Directions for Passenger Demand Analysis and Forecasting," Transportation Research, Vol. 1, No. 3 (1967), pp. 205-230.

C. H. Sharp, "The Choice Between Car and Bus on Urban Roads," Journal of Transport Economics and Policy, Vol. 1, No. 1 (1967).

has been no evidence that practitioners are building simultaneous equation models to estimate relative importances. This is true despite the fact that Econometric Theory clearly indicates that estimating the demand side to determine attribute importances while ignoring the supply side will, in general, yield inconsistent estimates of such importances.[4] The purpose of this work is to develop the supply side of such an importance estimation model. The demand side of the model has been discussed in detail elsewhere so that emphasis here is on developing and estimating representative supply equations.[5]

The mode choice decision process for which data was collected is the journey to work/mode choice decision. The following information was obtained via a five page, mailed questionnaire for the respondent's first and second choice mode: attribute satisfaction ratings based on the semantic differential for 15 different attributes (see Table I) and attribute values on seven quantitative attributes (see Table II).[6] As has been discussed elsewhere, the semantic differential has been used to obtain "attribute satisfaction ratings" as

---

[4]Arthur S. Goldberger, Econometric Theory (John Wiley & Sons, Inc., New York, 1964), pp. 192-194.

[5]James P. Wallace III, "Some Applications of Marketing Research Techniques to the New Mode Demand Forecasting Problem", Selected Proceedings of a Conference on Methods and Concepts of Forecasting Travel Demand for Future Transportation Systems (Transportation Studies Center, Center for Urban Research and Experiment, University of Pennsylvania, Philadelphia, Pennsylvania, April, 1972).

Alistair Sherret, "Structuring an Econometric Model of Modal Choice" (Dissertation: Cornell University, 1971).

James P. Wallace III and Alistair Sherret, "Estimating the Relative Importance of Product Attributes," Part I above.

[6]Charles E. Osgood, George J. Suci and Percy H. Tannenbaum, The Measurement of Meaning (University of Illinois Press, Urbana, Illinois, 1957).

opposed to attribute ratings by defining end points using terms like "very satisfied -- very unsatisfied."[7] The higher the rating, the more satisfied the respondent claimed to be regarding the particular mode attribute.

---

[7]Wallace, "Some Applications of Marketing Research Techniques to the New Mode Demand Forecasting Problem."

Sherret, "Structuring an Econometric Model of Modal Choice."

Wallace and Sherret, "Estimating the Relative Importance of Product Attributes," Part I above.

TABLE I

KEY TO ATTRIBUTE DESCRIPTIONS

(Attributes for which attribute satisfaction ratings given)

Attribute Number	Description[a]	Abbreviation
1	Comfort in Vehicle	Comfort
2	Dependability of On-Time Arrival	Dependability
3	Protection from Weather while Waiting	Weather
4	Frequency of Vehicle Departure Times	Frequency
5	Pleasantness of Trip	Pleasantness
6	Attractiveness of Vehicle	Attractiveness
7	Noise in Vehicle	Noise
8	Chance of Accidents	Accidents
9	Exposure to Undesirable Behavior of Others	Behavior
10	Traffic	Traffic
11	Bodily Crowding	Crowding
12	Out-of-pocket Cost of Trip	Cost
13	Total Time Spent Riding	Riding Time
14	Total Time Spent Walking	Walking Time
15	Total Time Spent Waiting	Waiting Time

[a]Attribute descriptions are those given in the questionnaire as labels for the semantic differential scales.

TABLE II

KEY TO ATTRIBUTE DESCRIPTIONS

(Attributes for which attribute values are given)

Attribute Number	Description	Units	Abbreviation
4	Vehicle Interdepature Times	minutes	Frequency
13	Total Time Spent Riding	minutes	Riding Time
14	Total Time Spent Walking	minutes	Walking Time
15	Total Time Spent Waiting	minutes	Waiting Time
16	Distance Travelled	miles (coded)	Distance
17	Daily Parking Cost	cents	Parking Cost
18	One-way Fare	cents	Fare

There was a total mailing of 10,000; approximately 1,000 were returned. The statistical results in this paper are for the subsample making the choice auto (driver or passenger) versus rail transit. The total sample was 117 (60 choosing auto, 57, transit). The demographic composition of this sample is shown in Table III. A detailed discussion of the questionnaire and its design is in the literature.[8]

[8] Thomas F. Golob, The Survey of User Choice of Alternate Transportation Modes, Research Publication GMR-950 (General Motors Research Laboratories, Warren, Michigan, January, 1970).

TABLE III

SAMPLE DEMOGRAPHIC COMPOSITION

Sex	
Male	83
Female	17
	100%

College Education	
None	28
1 to 3 years	21
4 or more years	51
	100%

AGE	
0-25	14
26-35	38
36-45	25
46-55	12
56-99	9
No Response	2
	100%

Annual Family Income	
$7000 and Under	9
$7000 - $10,000	23
$10,000 - $15,000	34
Over $15,000	32
No Response	2
	100%

2. Preliminary Estimation of the Demand Equation

Model 1

Given in Table IV are the results of the regression of y (a dummy variable indicating mode choice, 1 for auto, 0 for transit) on all fifteen observed relative attribute satisfaction ratings Q_i expressed as differences, auto versus transit.

TABLE IV

MODEL 1

$$y = a_0 + \sum_i a_i Q_i \qquad i = 1, 2, \ldots, 15$$

Explanatory Variable	Estimated Coefficient	t-statistic	Relative Coefficient
Q14 (Walking Time)	0.0745	3.650	1.000
Q2 (Dependability)	0.0530	2.611	0.703
Q6 (Attractiveness)	-0.0382	-1.445	-0.507
Q15 (Waiting Time)	0.0371	1.423	0.492
Q5 (Pleasantness)	0.0326	1.376	0.432
Q8 (Accidents)	0.0260	1.140	0.345
Q13 (Riding Time)	0.0257	1.139	0.340
Q11 (Crowding)	0.0170	0.774	0.226
Q7 (Noise)	-0.0152	-0.667	-0.202
Q10 (Traffic)	-0.0139	-0.618	-0.184
Q1 (Comfort)	-0.0091	-0.308	-0.121
Q12 (Cost)	0.0072	0.380	0.095
Q4 (Frequency)	0.0052	0.183	0.069
Q9 (Behavior)	-0.0038	-0.224	-0.050
Q3 (Weather)	0.0026	0.124	0.034

Constant $a_0 = 0.4765$

$S_y = 0.409$

$R^2 = 0.423$ Critical $t_{0.025, 101} = 1.984$

We may observe firstly from these that the coefficient estimates have generally very low associated null t-statistics. The critical t value is 1.984 at a 5% confidence level, and only Q14 (walking time) and Q2 (dependability) have associated t-statistics exceeding this critical value. Secondly, several coefficients have the "wrong" (i.e., negative) signs although none of these is highly significantly different from zero. It is commonplace for the regression coefficients to be termed importances, generally with no theoretical support.[9]

Elsewhere we have argued, on a theoretical basis, that the regression coefficients can be interpreted as importances.[10] The a priori expected, (i.e., "correct"), sign is positive for all variables since for every attribute we would expect an increase in the satisfaction with the automobile mode relative to the transit mode to result in an increased probability of automobile being chosen (other things remaining unchanged).

Thirdly, the attributes indicated as being most important (i.e., having the largest coefficients) in this model are generally the "time-related" attributes such as dependability, walking, waiting and riding time; the "comfort-related" attributes such as comfort and protection from the weather are apparently unimportant. Fourthly, the adjusted R^2 statistic of 0.432, while highly significant, does not indicate a particularly large proportion of the sample variance of y accounted for by the regression. However, given the diverse nature of the demographic composition of the sample, as shown in Table III, the fit appears reasonable. It should also be noted that semantic differential yields integer values (here 1 through 7) which also lowers the maximum potential fit.

In view of the large number of variables included in the regression and the high collinearities between many of them, the problems

---

[9] James H. Myers and Mark I. Alpert, "Determining Buying Attitudes: Meaning and Measurement," Journal of Marketing, Vol. 32 (October, 1968), pp. 13-20.

[10] Wallace, "Some Applications of Marketing Research Techniques to the New Mode Demand Forecasting Problem."

Sherret and Wallace, "Estimating the Relative Importance of Product Attributes," Part I above.

of unreliability of the coefficients should not be altogether surprising. One third of the elements to the right of the principle diagonal of the correlation matrix were statistically significant at the 5% level. Multicollinearity, that is, high linear correlations between the independent variables of a regression, has the effect of increasing the standard errors of the coefficients and so reduces their statistical significance.[11] Some of this multicollinearity is caused by semantic redundancy among the attributes and some is due to supply side relationships. This problem was discussed in detail in Part I of this work.[12] Here our objective is to mitigate the semantic redundancy problem.

Applying factor analysis to the relative attribute satisfaction variables, the original fifteen attributes may be replaced by a smaller set of variables which adequately represents the dimensionality in the original sample space and which forms a meaningful set of modal choice decision variables. Nine components accounted for 88% of the total sample variance. A set of nine original variables was chosen to represent each of the first nine principal components. In order to reduce multicollinearity, these nine variables were taken as the explanatory variables for the regression given below as Model 2.

Model 2

The results given in Table V for the nine-variable model are subject to comments similar to those made for Model 1. The t-statistics again indicate generally low reliability for the coefficient estimates in spite of the removal of some of the highly collinear variables; Q14 (walking time) and Q2 (dependability) are again the only

---

[11] Goldberger, Econometric Theory.

[12] See Part I, Sections 6 - 9.

variables whose coefficient estimates are significantly different from zero at the 5% level although Q15 (waiting time) is indicated as having a coefficient significant at a 6% level. The coefficients for Q1 (comfort) and Q9 (behavior) have the "wrong" signs although neither is highly significantly different from zero, and as before, the "time-related" variables appear to be of dominant importance in the regression. Finally, note that adjusted R^2 is reduced to 0.38.

TABLE V

MODEL 2

$$y = a_0 + \sum_i a_i Q_i \qquad i = 1,2,3,9,10,12,13,14,15$$

Explanatory Variable	Estimated Coefficient	t-statistic	Relative Coefficient
Q14 (Walking Time)	0.0703	3.490	1.000
Q2 (Dependability)	0.0561	2.812	0.798
Q15 (Waiting Time)	0.0453	1.926	0.645
Q13 (Riding Time)	0.0276	1.228	0.392
Q1 (Comfort)	-0.0202	-0.983	-0.288
Q12 (Cost)	0.0151	0.825	0.215
Q10 (Traffic)	0.0071	0.355	0.101
Q3 (Weather)	0.0034	0.170	0.048
Q9 (Behavior)	-0.0032	-0.229	-0.045

Constant $a_0 = 0.4718$

$S_y = 0.412$

$R^2 = 0.380$ Critical $t_{0.025,107} = 1.982$

Model 3

In Table VI are given the results of the regression of y on the five variables Q2, Q12, Q13, Q14 and Q15. These five were selected because they have the largest (positive) coefficient estimates of the variables included in Model 2, and were thus implied to be the most important in that model, although in Model 2 variables Q12 (cost) and Q13 (riding time) have coefficients significantly different from zero only at confidence levels 42% and 22% respectively.

The results of Model 3 show the coefficients of Q14 (walking time), Q2 (dependability) and Q15 (waiting time) to be significant at the 5% level and those of Q12 (cost) and Q13 (riding time) to be significant only at much lower confidence levels. Coefficients having "wrong" signs have been eliminated in Model 3 and the adjusted R^2 is 0.372. The five relative attribute satisfaction variables included in Model 3 are assumed for the purposes of subsequent analysis in this work to be the relevant explanatory variables of the demand side relationship. This assumption is based both on the regression results just discussed and on a priori grounds due to the findings of other researchers reviewed later. Accordingly, the coefficient values of Model 3, expressed relative to that of Q14 (walking time), are taken as the "relative importance" estimates to be used as a basis for comparison with subsequent results based on the estimation of a simultaneous equation model.

TABLE VI

MODEL 3

$$y = a_0 + \sum_i a_i Q_i \qquad i = 2, 12, 13, 14, 15$$

Explanatory Variable	Estimated Coefficient	t-statistic	Relative Coefficient
Q14 (Walking Time)	0.0706	3.569	1.000
Q2 (Dependability)	0.0525	2.712	0.744
Q15 (Waiting Time)	0.0447	2.063	0.633
Q13 (Riding Time)	0.0233	1.139	0.330
Q12 (Cost)	0.0152	0.884	0.216

Constant $a_0 = 0.4141$

$S_y = 0.407$

$R^2 = 0.372$ Critical $t_{0.025,111} = 1.981$

Two objections may be made to the selection of only the five variables of Model 3 for further estimation. The first is that exclusion of the other attributes on the basis of their low "importance" in the single equation Models 1 and 2 should be, strictly speaking, regarded as an inconsistency in the logic of simultaneous equation model construction since we do not believe that the relative importance estimates of a single equation model are consistent. The possibility then arises that some attribute which is in fact important and whose importance would be recognized if it were included in a properly specified simultaneous equation model is excluded from consideration. While this remains a possibility in the model, it was felt that the highly insignificant coefficients associated with the excluded variables made unlikely their entry into the demand side of a more structured model in a significant way. Further, the five selected variables, even if an "incomplete" set of modal descriptors, form in themselves a useful basis for comparison.

The second objection is that all the included variables except dependability are time- or cost-related "quantitative" attribute variables; "qualitative" attributes such as comfort, noise, and protection from the weather are omitted since their coefficients are insignificant in Models 1 and 2. In order to further investigate the contribution of these "qualitative" attribute variables to the modal choice, y was regressed on just the seven attribute variables which might be described as "qualitative." This regression is designated Model 4.

<u>Model 4</u>

Details of the regression are given in Table VII. Of the seven relative attribute satisfaction variables included, only Q5 (pleasantness) is indicated as having a coefficient significantly different from zero at the 5% level, while Q11 (crowding) and Q6 (attractiveness) are significant at the 10% level, and the remaining coefficients are highly insignificant. The generally low t-statistics are to be expected given the high collinearities which exist between many of these variables. Variables Q6 (attractiveness), Q9 (behavior), and Q1 (comfort) also have the "wrong" sign. The adjusted R^2 for the regression is 0.18. One of the problems here that is often overlooked is that these qualitative attributes often mean different things to a respondent depending on the mode being rated. Further discussions of this problem and its resolution are outside the scope of this work.

TABLE VII

MODEL 4

$$y = a_0 + \sum_i a_i Q_i \qquad i = 1, 3, 5, 6, 7, 9, 11$$

Explanatory Variable	Estimated Coefficient	t-statistic	Relative Coefficient
Q5 (Pleasantness)	0.0781	3.409	1.000
Q6 (Attractiveness)	-0.0502	-1.718	-0.643
Q11 (Crowding)	0.0425	1.817	0.544
Q1 (Comfort)	-0.0151	-0.464	-0.193
Q9 (Behavior)	-0.0082	-0.480	-0.105
Q7 (Noise)	0.0023	0.093	0.030
Q3 (Weather)	0.0668	0.311	0.087

Constant $a_0 = 0.4497$

$S_y = 0.469$

$R^2 = 0.180$ Critical $t_{0.025, 109} = 1.982$

Bearing in mind the uncertainties (including the objections just mentioned) associated with the estimates of these importances, the results suggest that for the journey to work, travellers make their mode choice primarily on the basis of the "quantitative" attributes of the journey with little regard for the "qualitative" attributes, indicating that for most individuals getting to work on-time and in as short a time as possible are the over-riding concerns. This is a result which we would not necessarily expect to hold true for non-work trips. It should be remembered that these and any other similar inferences about attribute importances are conditional on the range of attribute levels currently experienced by travellers, that is, parameter estimates are conditional on the data set used to calibrate the model. Here we are dealing with data obtained from relatively well-off Chicago suburbanites making a choice between auto and rail transit, and none of the respondents was considered captive to either mode.

3. Supply Side Formulation

To this point the modal choice model has been expressed in terms of a single "demand" equation. However, it has been argued that the data which must be used to estimate the model was "generated" by the simultaneous solution of demand and supply relationships. Estimation of the single equation demand model from such data, while ignoring the supply side, is consequently likely to yield statistically biased and inconsistent estimates of the relative importances, and these estimates may be highly misleading. Below it will be shown that this turned out to be the case in the illustrative example cited here. Theory dictates that in order to obtain consistent estimates of the importances, the relevant supply side relationships must be included in the structure of the model, and the model must be estimated via one of the techniques appropriate for estimating systems of simultaneous equations. A discussion of these techniques is outside the scope of this work. Goldberger provides an excellent reference textbook.[13]

---

[13]Goldberger, Econometric Theory.

It is important to note that even though the data is taken via questioning travellers regarding each of the two modes considered, certain of the attribute values are related to other attribute values because of supply considerations. (Note that presumably we have removed the semantic redundancy problems.) The modal choice process is viewed as a system of simultaneous relationships: Traveller-specific demand side relationships and mode-specific supply side relationships are considered together to determine modal choice as an equilibrium solution of the system. A flow diagram of the system is shown in Figure 1.

FIGURE 1

EQUILIBRIUM SYSTEM OF RELATIONSHIPS UNDERLYING AUTOMOBILE/RAIL TRANSIT MODAL CHOICE

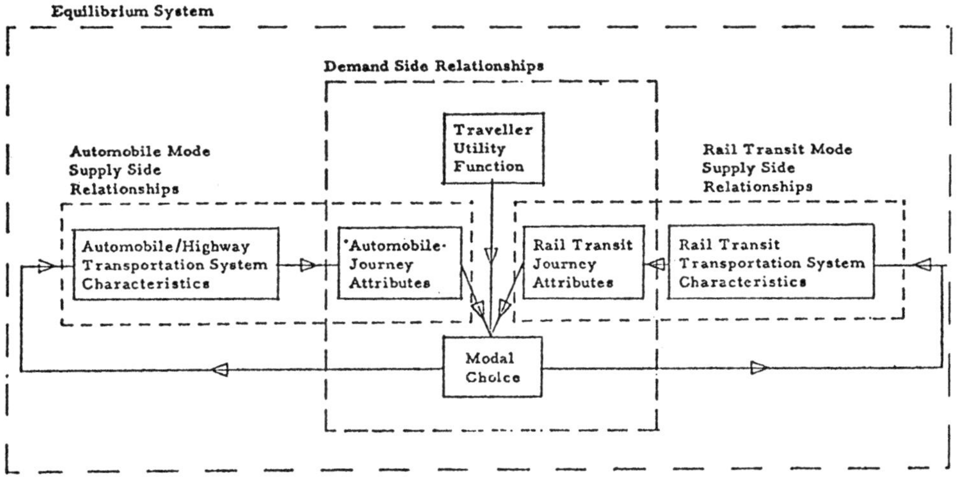

We are concerned next with hypothesizing separately the supply side relationships existing for the automobile and rail transit modes (which are depicted as subsystems in Figure 1). However, before beginning, it is worth noting on what basis such relationships may be estimated. In estimating demand relationships it is common to treat the data as a sample of observations from a population of travellers that could be thought of in terms of a representative traveller from the population. The demand equation is then developed on a theoretical basis to describe the representative traveller's behavior and used to predict overall mode split.

By analogy we can treat the same data set as a sample of observations from the population of node pairs between which travel by auto and transit occur. Supply relationships can then be developed separately for auto and transit for a representative node pair. Supply relationships are then hypothesized to exist, e.g., that riding time for auto is a function of distance, traffic, etc.

To completely close the system (see Figure 1) we note that changes in overall mode split will affect volume on each mode and, therefore, traffic. However, since this data set was taken at one point in time when the system is presumed to be in (near) equilibrium, this feedback loop relationship must be estimated separately. Alternatively, traffic may be treated as exogenous and adjusted as deemed necessary for model simulation purposes. The latter approach has been taken here but the authors feel that this is a shortcoming.

4. The Automobile/Highway Supply Side Model

The supply side relationships between the characteristics of the automobile/highway transportation system and the attributes of a journey by automobile would seem to arise, conceptually at least, in a fairly straightforward way as suggested in Figure 2. The transportation system characteristics listed on the left of the figure are assumed exogenous. As discussed above, highway volume and congestion (traffic) are specified as exogenous variables.

FIGURE 2

AUTOMOBILE MODE SUPPLY SIDE RELATIONSHIPS

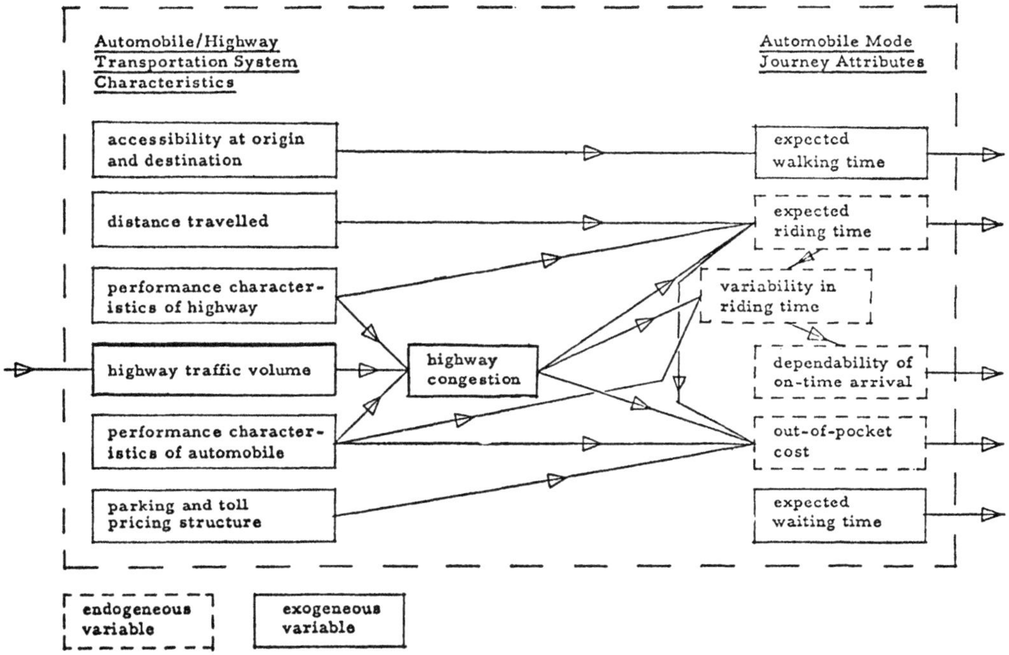

Reading the figure from left to right, the traffic volume, the performance characteristics of the highway (the so-called volume-capacity relationships), and the performance characteristics of the automobile such as speed and acceleration together determine the level of traffic congestion on the highway. Highway congestion in turn affects the expected riding time, the variability in riding time, and the out-of-pocket "running" cost of the automobile. The expected riding time also depends directly on highway performance characteristics such as the speed limits (in the absence of congestion), and, of course, on the distance travelled. The variability in riding time may be considered to depend directly on the reliability of performance characteristics of the automobile as well as on congestion and expected riding time. Out-of-pocket cost depends on the expected riding time, the performance (fuel consumption) characteristics of the automobile, parking and toll charges, and congestion.

The variability in riding time and dependability of on-time arrival are taken to be identical attributes in the model. Underlying this identity are the assumptions that the dependability of on-time arrival is equivalent to the variability or variance of total travel time and that the variance in the waiting and walking portions of the trip is negligible. It is not immediately obvious what is meant by waiting time for the automobile mode, presumably it is considered to be zero by most travellers since its satisfaction ratings were very high. However, it was included in the model (as an exogenous variable) since in relative terms (i.e., for demand side considerations), a zero attribute level is meaningful. Expected walking time is also included as an exogenous variable since it depends only on the exogenously specified accessibilities at origin and destination.

We may now summarize the automobile supply side dependencies in Figure 2 in the following forms:

<u>Automobile Mode</u>

$$(4.1)\qquad \text{dependability of on-time arrival} = f_1 \left\{ \begin{array}{l} \text{highway congestion} \\ \text{expected riding time} \\ \text{performance characteristics of automobile} \end{array} \right\}$$

Automobile Mode

$$(4.2) \quad \text{out-of-pocket cost} = f_2 \left\{ \begin{array}{l} \text{highway congestion} \\ \text{expected riding time} \\ \text{performance characteristics of automobile} \\ \text{parking and toll pricing structure} \end{array} \right\}$$

$$(4.3) \quad \text{expected riding time} = f_3 \left\{ \begin{array}{l} \text{highway congestion} \\ \text{distance travelled} \\ \text{performance characteristics of highway} \end{array} \right\}$$

The above relationships disregarded the limitations of data availability. We now specify the automobile supply side relations in terms of variables for which we have measurements. One such set of relationships corresponding to those given in equations (4.1), (4.2) and (4.3) is as follows:

$$(4.4) \quad \text{QA2 (dependability)} = f'_1 \left(\begin{array}{l} \text{QA10 (traffic)} \\ \text{XA13 (riding time)} \end{array} \right)$$

$$(4.5) \quad \text{QA12 (cost)} = f'_2 \left(\begin{array}{l} \text{QA10 (traffic)} \\ \text{XA13 (riding time)} \\ \text{XA17 (parking cost)} \end{array} \right)$$

$$(4.6) \quad \text{QA13 (riding time)} = f'_3 \left(\begin{array}{l} \text{QA10 (traffic)} \\ \text{XA16 (distance)} \end{array} \right)$$

The following notation has been used to define variables. The first letter is either a "Q" or an "X". A "Q" indicates the variable was measured via the semantic differential, as listed in Table I, while an "X" indicates the variable was measured directly as shown in Table II.

The second letter, either A or T, indicates auto or transit. The number indicates the attribute.

We may observe in comparing these relationships with those above, that as a result of the unavailability of appropriate data, no measures describing the performance characteristics of either the automobile or highway are included.

The attribute satisfaction rating QA10 (traffic) is included in the relationships as the best available measure of highway congestion. With regard to the inclusion of variable QA10 recall that (ideally) the supply side relationships should be specified in terms of the actual (as opposed to perceived) values of attributes rather than in terms of satisfaction ratings since the supply side is defined to exist between the attributes of the mode, independent of traveller preferences. Thus, we would specify the relationships entirely in terms of attribute values if this were possible. But, it is not, since we can obtain measures of qualitative attributes only in terms of satisfaction ratings; we consequently make use of the attribute satisfaction variables obtained via the semantic differential.

Table VIII shows linear supply equation estimates for the automobile mode. The adjusted R^2 statistics of 0.34 for equation LA2 (dependability), 0.42 for equation LA12 (cost) and 0.54 for LA13 (riding time) are all highly significant; all coefficient estimates are of the a priori expected sign, and with the exception of the XA13 (riding time) variable in equation LA12, all coefficient estimates are significantly different from zero at the 5% confidence level. The fact that perceived out-of-pocket cost is indicated as not depending significantly on the expected time spent riding is interesting insofar as it suggests that automobile mileage or running costs under uncongested road conditions may not be an important component of perceived

TABLE VIII

LINEAR SUPPLY EQUATION ESTIMATES

AUTOMOBILE MODE

Equation LA2 (Automobile Dependability)

$QA2 = c_0 + c_1 QA10 + c_2 XA13$

Explanatory Variable	Estimated Coefficient	t-statistic
QA10 (Traffic)	0.2642	2.776
XA13 (Riding Time)	-0.0437	-4.799

Constant $c_0 = 5.5835$

$S_y = 1.653$ Critical $R^2 = 0.050$

$R^2 = 0.336$ Critical $t_{0.025, 114} = 1.981$

Equation LA12 (Automobile Cost)

$QA12 = c_0 + c_1 QA10 + c_2 XA13 + c_3 XA17$

Explanatory Variable	Estimated Coefficient	t-statistic
QA10 (Traffic)	0.5627	5.846
XA13 (Riding Time)	-0.0072	-0.758
XA17 (Parking Cost)	-0.0062	-3.757

Constant $c_0 = 3.3983$

$S_y = 1.669$ Critical $R^2 = 0.065$

$R^2 = 0.415$ Critical $t_{0.025, 113} = 1.981$

Equation LA13 (Automobile Riding Time)

$QA13 = c_0 + c_1 QA10 + c_2 XA16$

Explanatory Variable	Estimated Coefficient	t-statistic
QA10 (Traffic)	0.6419	8.624
XA16 (Distance)	-0.5128	-4.669

Constant $c_0 = 4.2987$

$S_y = 1.418$ Critical $R^2 = 0.050$

$R^2 = 0.536$ Critical $t_{0.025, 114} = 1.981$

out-of-pocket cost. On the other hand, the high significance of the "traffic" variable coefficient indicates that running costs under congested, stop-and-go driving conditions are perceived as a significant component of out-of-pocket cost. All in all, these results provide an encouraging validation of the supply relationships hypothesized to exist for the automobile mode.

5. The Rail Transit Supply Side Model

Figure 3 shows the supply side relationships hypothesized to exist between the rail transit transportation system characteristics and the journey attributes of the rail transit mode. The transportation system characteristics are specified to be exogenous. The degree of passenger congestion (bodily crowding) as determined by the passenger volume and the performance characteristics of the rail system is treated as exogenous.

It is assumed that dependability of on-time arrival can be identified with the variance of waiting time and the variance of riding time. As with the automobile mode, the variance of walking time is assumed to be negligible. Both the expected value and variance of waiting time are affected by passenger congestion since, as the arrival rate of passengers approaches and exceeds the service rate provided by departing vehicles, queues will develop and grow. The expected value and variance of waiting time also depend on the frequency of vehicle departures, the number of transfers between vehicles and the reliability of performance of the transit system.

FIGURE 3

RAIL TRANSIT MODE SUPPLY SIDE RELATIONSHIPS

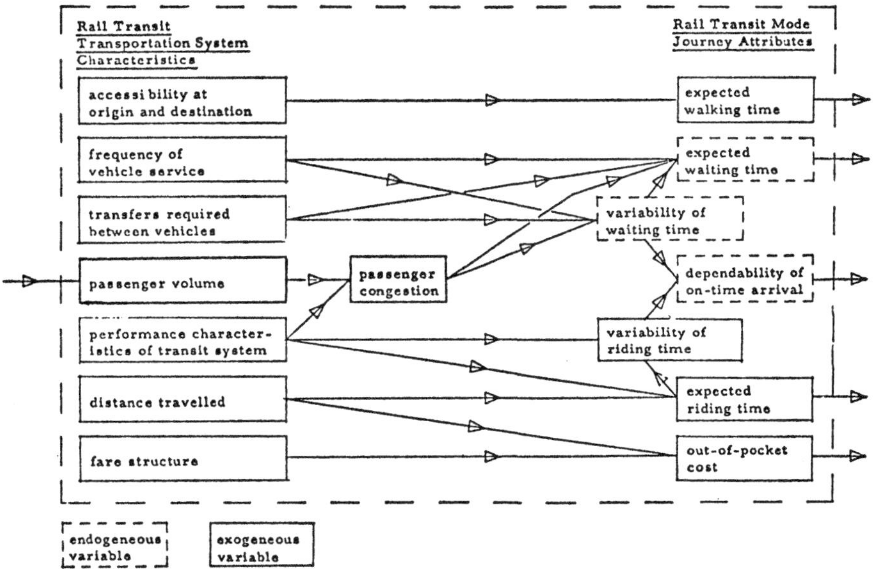

A further dependency exists between the expected value of waiting time and its variability. Consider, for example, a simple rail journey between origin and destination stations where no transfers are required so that waiting time is experienced only at the origin station. Expected waiting would be essentially zero if the vehicle departures were "perfectly" dependable (and of sufficient capacity). This is to say if a traveller knew in advance exactly when his train were to depart, he would presumably plan to arrive at the origin station just in time to board the train without having to wait. However, in the more usual case, vehicles are not perfectly dependable and this fact causes expected waiting time to be greater than zero.

The variability of riding time is dependent on the expected value of riding time since the longer the trip the more likely may be the chance of delays. The expected values of riding time and walking time are considered exogenous, as is out-of-pocket cost. With regard to the latter, we may note that the relationships we have considered emphasize the congestion effects on the supply side. These, however, are not as obviously the most important relationships as was the case for the automobile supply side, and, in general, it may be supposed that other important supply side relationships exist, particularly the "cost" supply relations which underlie the fare structure. We may note, however, that for the rail transit system considered in this study, the fare structure was to a large extent "fixed"; (i.e., for large variations in travel distance the fare was constant). We are, hence, justified in treating out-of-pocket cost as an exogenous variable.

We may now summarize the rail transit supply side relationships given in Figure 3 in the following forms:

<u>Rail Transit Mode</u>

(5.1) dependability of on-time arrival $= f_4$ {passenger congestion; frequency of vehicle service; transfers required between vehicles; expected riding time; performance characteristics of transit system}

Rail Transit Mode

$$(5.2) \quad \text{expected waiting time} = f_5 \left\{ \begin{array}{l} \text{passenger congestion} \\ \text{frequency of vehicle service} \\ \text{transfers required between vehicles} \\ \text{variability of waiting time} \end{array} \right\}$$

We may now propose transit supply relationships between variables for which we have data. One pair of relations corresponding to equations (5.1) and (5.2) which may be specified is the following:

$$(5.3) \quad \text{QT2 (dependability)} = f'_4 \left(\begin{array}{l} \text{QT11 (crowding)} \\ \text{XT14 (frequency)} \\ \text{XT13 (riding time)} \end{array} \right)$$

$$(5.4) \quad \text{QT15 (waiting time)} = f'_5 \left(\begin{array}{l} \text{QT11 (crowding)} \\ \text{XT4 (frequency)} \\ \text{QT2 (dependability)} \end{array} \right)$$

We may note firstly that QT11 (crowding) is taken as the proxy for passenger congestion, and secondly that performance characteristics of the system for which we have no measures are excluded. Note also that QT2 (dependability) is taken as a proxy variable for variability of waiting time. This is justified to the extent that the variability in waiting time is large compared to the variability in riding time.

Linear supply equations were estimated for the rail transit mode and the results are given in Table IX. For both equations LT2 (dependability) and LT15 (waiting time), the adjusted R^2 statistics (of 0.21 and 0.58 respectively) are highly significant. All coefficient estimates have the correct sign and are significant at a 5% confidence level, (with the exception of the coefficient of XT13 (riding time) in equation LT2 which is significant at a 7% level). Thus, it would appear that dependability is affected most by variability in waiting time as opposed to variability in riding time which makes it reasonable to use it as a proxy variable for the former. Once again it would appear that reasonable supply side relationships can be validated utilizing the data set gathered from consumers and, hence, cannot be ignored.

TABLE IX

LINEAR SUPPLY EQUATION ESTIMATES

RAIL TRANSIT MODE

Equation LT2 (Transit Dependability)

$$QT2 = c_0 + c_1 QT11 + c_2 XT4 + c_3 XT13$$

Explanatory Variable	Estimated Coefficient	t-statistic
QT11 (Crowding)	0.3435	4.930
XT4 (Frequency)	-0.0323	-2.310
XT13 (Riding Time)	-0.0160	-1.654

Constant $c_0 = 4.8726$

$S_y = 1.596$ Critical $R^2 = 0.065$

$R^2 = 0.209$ Critical $t_{0.025, 113} = 1.981$

Equation LT15 (Transit Waiting Time)

$$QT15 = c_0 + c_1 QT11 + c_2 QT2 + c_3 XT4.$$

Explanatory Variable	Estimated Coefficient	t-statistic
QT11 (Crowding)	0.1773	3.303
QT2 (Dependability)	0.5907	9.083
XT4 (Frequency)	-0.0220	-2.196

Constant $c_0 = 1.8275$

$S_y = 1.117$ Critical $R^2 = 0.065$

$R^2 = 0.575$ Critical $t_{0.025, 113} = 1.981$

6. A Simultaneous Equation Model

Combining the demand relationship of Model 3 with the five supply relationships discussed in the preceding section, we may define now our simultaneous equation model as:

(6.1) $$y = a_0 + a_2 Q2 + a_{12} Q12 + a_{13} Q13 + a_{14} Q14 + a_{15} Q15$$

(6.2) $$QA2 = c_{10} + c_{11} QA10 + c_{12} XA13$$

(6.3) $$QA12 = c_{20} + c_{21} QA10 + c_{22} XA13 + c_{23} XA17$$

(6.4) $$QA13 = c_{30} + c_{31} QA10 + c_{32} XA16$$

(6.5) $$QT2 = c_{40} + c_{41} QT11 + c_{42} XT13 + c_{43} XT4$$

(6.6) $$QT15 = c_{50} + c_{51} QT11 + c_{52} QT2 + c_{53} XT4$$

(6.7) $$Q2 = QA2 - QT2$$

(6.8) $$Q12 = QA12 - QT12$$

(6.9) $$Q13 = QA13 - QT13$$

(6.10) $$Q15 = QA15 - QT15$$

which we wish to estimate in order to obtain consistent estimates of the coefficients a_i of equation (6.1). Equation (6.1) is the "single equation" demand relationship of Model 3. Equations (6.2), (6.3), and (6.4) are respectively the automobile supply relationships LA2 (dependability), LA12 (cost), and LA13 (riding time). Equations (6.5) and (6.6) are the rail transit supply relationships LT2 (dependability) and LT15 (waiting time). Finally, equations (6.7), (6.8), (6.9), and (6.10) are simply identities providing the links between the demand and supply sides.

On the supply side the variables QA2, QA12, QA13, QT2, and QT15 are specified to be endogenous and the remainder are exogenous. In the demand relationship the left-hand variable y, the probability of choosing auto is endogenous; the right-hand variable Q14 is exogenous, and the right-hand variables Q2, Q12, Q13, and Q15 are determined from the endogenous variables of the supply side relationships together with the exogenously specified variables QT12, QT13, and QA15 through the "linkage" identities.

It should be noted that the model can be transformed into a recursive form entailing five endogenous variables and all relationships are identified. If feedback equations linking auto traffic and transit crowding to y would have been used the model would no longer have been recursive. However, although our equation system has a recursive form, there is no reason to suppose that the system is diagonal, (i.e., that the disturbance term of equation (6.1) is independent of the disturbance terms of the supply side relations). In fact, our arguments on the simultaneity of the supply and demand relationships in the modal choice decision would dictate that this is not so. Two stage least squares yields consistent estimates of the parameters of equation (6.1) and was used here.[14] The results of the estimation of this model, which is denoted Model 5, are given in Table X.

---

[14] Goldberger, Econometric Theory, pp. 329-336.

TABLE X

MODEL 5

Demand with Automobile and Transit Supply Relations

$$y = a_0 + a_{14}Q14 + a_2\hat{Q}2 + a_{15}\hat{Q}15 + a_{13}\hat{Q}13 + a_{12}\hat{Q}12$$

where
$$\hat{Q}2 = \hat{Q}A2 - \hat{Q}T2$$
$$\hat{Q}15 = QA15 - \hat{Q}T15$$
$$\hat{Q}13 = \hat{Q}A13 - QT13$$
$$\hat{Q}12 = \hat{Q}A12 - QT12$$

Explanatory Variable	Estimated Coefficient	t-statistic	Relative Coefficient
Q14 (Walking Time)	.0853	4.606	1.000
Q2 (Dependability)	.1140	3.584	1.336
Q15 (Waiting Time)	.0568	2.500	0.666
Q13 (Riding Time)	.0670	2.581	0.785
Q12 (Cost)	-.0351	-1.596	-0.411

Constant $a_0 = 0.4187$

$S_y = 0.386$

$R^2 = 0.433$ Critical $t_{0.025,111} = 1.981$

The point of principal interest here is the comparison of the results of Model 3 (the single equation demand model) with those of Model 5 (the simultaneous equation model). Summarized in Table XI are the coefficient estimates for these two models expressed relative to the coefficient of Q14 (walking time). The relative coefficient values or relative importances given in parentheses are indicated by their associated t-statistics as not being significantly different from zero at the 5% confidence level. Also given are the adjusted R^2 statistics for the demand equation.

TABLE XI

RELATIVE IMPORTANCES

Variable	Model 3	Model 5
Q14 (walking time)	1.000	1.000
Q2 (Dependability)	0.744	1.336
Q15 (Waiting time)	0.633	0.666
Q13 (Riding time)	(0.330)	0.785
Q12 (Cost)	(0.216)	(-0.411)
R^2 Statistic	0.372	0.433

Clearly, introduction of the supply relationships substantially changes the relative importance estimates. Note especially the change in the relative importance of "dependability of on-time arrival" from 0.7 in Model 3 to 1.3 in Model 5, and the change in the value for "riding time" from 0.3 (which was statistically insignificant) in Model 3 to a statistically significant 0.8 in Model 5. The relative importance of "waiting time" does not change much and the importance of "out-of-pocket cost" is insignificant in both models. Note also that the R^2 statistic is higher for Model 5 than for Model 3, indicating that in terms of the variance of the data explained, it is a "better" model. Kloek has demonstrated that in comparing two models we may be increasingly confident that the model with the smaller R^2 is incorrectly specified as sample sizes become large.[15] It may be noted also that the R^2 of 0.433 from Model 5 is even higher than the

[15] T. Kloek and L. E. M. Mennes, "Simultaneous Estimation Based on Principal Components of Predetermined Variables," Econometrica, Vol. 28 (January, 1960), pp. 45-61.

R^2 of 0.423 for Model 1, the single equation demand model which included all 15 attributes.

We may conclude from the relative importances resulting from Model 5 given in Table XI that, for the population of travellers sampled (generally high income) and the mode pair selected, dependability of on-time arrival is the most important modal attribute in determining an individual's choice of mode for the daily journey to work. The total time spent walking is the next most important attribute, followed in importance by the total time spent riding and the total time spent waiting. The out-of-pocket cost did not seem to be a significant consideration. Remember that "comfort" type attributes were previously found to be of little importance.

Given that we are considering modal choice for the work trip, the high importances attached to the dependability of on-time arrival and expected travel time, and the low importances attached to the comfort type aspects of the trip might be expected. The indicated unimportance of out-of-pocket cost is at first sight perhaps less easy to accept, but it should be noted, we are here dealing with a sample of travellers having a high average income (about 70% over $10,000) so that it is to be expected that the differences in variable costs between auto and transit will be of less importance to our sample than they would to a group having lower incomes.

7. Comparison of Results

While recognizing the generally low statistical reliability of our attribute importance estimates, it is interesting to compare them where possible with the results obtained in other studies. This is somewhat difficult; firstly, because of the lack of rigorously or consistently defined measures of importance in these studies; secondly, because of the variations in attribute definitions used; and thirdly, because of the inclusion of only the quantitative variables of time and cost in most of the studies.

The "attitudinal" approach of Paine et al. is, in fact, the only study we have considered in which a comprehensive attempt was made to include qualitative attributes.[16] Here the "importances" of a large number of attributes were measured directly via the semantic differential technique. Factor analysis was then used to group the attributes into a small number of factors and the importance of each factor computed by taking the mean of the scaled responses for all attributes included in the factor (on the basis of their varimax rotated factor scores). The factors derived by this method, listed in order of their importance in the choice between auto and transit for the work trip, are as follows: Most important was the "reliability of destination achievement" factor included in which were attributes describing the chance of accidents, the necessity of stopping for repairs, and the safety of the vehicle. The second most important factor was "travel time" included in which were attributes describing both the expected value of travel time and the dependability of on-time arrival. Third most important was a "weather" factor describing both the extent to which the vehicle performance is affected by the weather and the protection from the weather while waiting. Next most important was the cost factor, followed by comfort and convenience-related factors. In this purely attitudinal approach to importance estimation, importances were determined without reference to the modal choices actually made by the individuals or to their satisfaction with the current attribute levels. Further, we have little idea of the statistical

---

[16] Frank T. Paine, Allan N. Nash, Stanley J. Hille and Allen G. Brunner, "Consumer Attitudes Toward Auto Versus Public Transport Alternatives".

reliability of the results; nevertheless, the results of Paine et al. provide a useful basis for comparison with our own. Differences in the definitions of the factors and attributes make direct comparison difficult, but it is interesting that the results of Paine et al. are basically similar to ours insofar as dependability, travel time, and waiting time factors are of greatest importance, and cost and comfort factors are less important.

Another attitudinal study which made an attempt to measure the relative importance of qualitative attributes and whose results will be summarized here is that of the University of Pennsylvania.[17] Using a direct questionnaire technique, the relative "sensitivity" of the individuals to the attributes of cost, time, comfort and convenience was measured. In the modal choice for work and school trips, 33% of the sample were classified as being most sensitive to time, 23% as being most sensitive to comfort, 15% to cost, and 15% to convenience. The broad and imprecise definitions of the attributes together with the approximate nature of the research preclude much meaningful comparison of these results with our own beyond the agreement that time is indicated as being of greatest importance and cost of minor importance. Our results appear to be in general agreement with the attitudinal studies reviewed.

Among the "inferential" studies which we reviewed, the attributes included were, with one minor exception, confined to relative monetary cost and the relative expected monetary values of the components of total travel time. By implication, in those studies where the objective was to determine a "value" for time, cost is considered to be of significant importance. Lave, in fact, using standardized regression

---

[17] Individual Preferences for Various Means of Transportation Management Science Center, University of Pennsylvania, (May, 1965).

coefficients as his measures of relative importance, determined the cost difference to be the most important variable in his basic model with comfort (measured as a dummy variable) and time as the next most important.[18] Cost plays a lesser, although still generally a significant, role in other models. Relative travel time is in all cases inferred to be a highly significant determinant of modal choice, and where in-vehicle time and walking and waiting times (the latter two frequently combined as so-called "excess" time) are included as separate variables, unit excess time is inferred to be more "valuable" than riding time. In none of these inferential modal choice models was it attempted to include a measure of the variability of travel time or dependability of on-time arrival.

In these inferential models, auto costs are often estimated as a function of distance plus parking fees and tolls. We have shown that, for both auto and transit, the time-related attributes are often correlated due to supply side relationships. Estimating costs as a function of distance will make cost correlated to the time variables as well.

Failure to take these supply side relationships into consideration is likely to lead to estimates of relative importances which leave much to be desired. In fact, it is not surprising to us that our results agree more closely with those of the attitudinal studies than those of previous single equation inferential approaches.

At any rate, there should be little doubt that correlations due to supply side phenomena are generally strong enough so that reasonable supply side relationships can be estimated. There should also be little doubt that in this case the relative importance estimates will vary considerably depending on whether the supply side is introduced

---

[18] Lave, "A Behavioral Approach to Modal Split Forecasting."

into the model.

It should also be noted that the comparison of the results of different models is particularly hazardous when the data used involves different transportation systems.

8. Conclusions

We would like it clearly understood that we found our importance estimates to be extremely sensitive to supply side model structure. The model was in no way robust in this regard, and we found this to be a very discouraging finding. We hope that further work in progress using larger samples alleviates this problem.

At this point, it should be clear that a simultaneous equation importance estimation model is mode-pair specific. This feature makes handling new modes difficult although, we feel, not impossible. But it does make the development, estimation, validation and implementation of such models very time consuming and expensive. It should be recognized that, after more than two decades and the expenditure of millions, the simultaneous equation macroeconomic models are still far from perfect. In fact, a very recent article argues that in some instances a single (reduced form) equation model out forecasts the larger simultaneous equation macroeconomic models.[19] Frequently this is due to the confounding effects of model specification errors when simultaneous equation estimation methods, such as two stage least squares, are used.

In fact, there is currently a difference of opinion among many builders of large macroeconomic models as to how the models should be estimated (not simulated). One school opting for procedures such as

---

[19] Yoel Haitovsky and George Treyz, "Forecasts with Quarterly Macro-econometric Models, Equation Adjustments, and Benchmark Predictions: The U. S. Experience", The Review of Economics and Statistics, Vol. 54, No. 3 (August, 1972), pp. 317-325.

two stage least squares and the other vying for direct least squares claiming that due to the effects of specification error, it is to be preferred. There is certainly some question about the proper specification of the supply side of mode choice models. A problem aggravated by actual versus perceived attributes and measurement difficulties for qualitative attributes. Hence, one might, therefore, argue that direct least squares on the demand equation is appropriate. Model 3 importance estimates would be the result. The supply equations would also be estimated via direct least squares.

However, econometric model builders would argue that conditional forecasts of the effects on mode choice of changes in mode attributes would still have to be done in the context of the full system of simultaneous equations (i.e., using the appropriate reduced form equations) rather than via the single demand equation given in Model 3. In short, regardless of how the model is estimated, it is appropriate to do the model simulation in terms of the entire system of equations. Keep in mind that the sole reason for estimating importances is to facilitate conditional forecasting.

Moreover, before successful simulation with simultaneous equation mode choice models can proceed, the overall fits of the equations must be improved considerably. Demographic stratification, larger samples and improved supply relationships may help. However, we will also need to do additional work on the feedback equations so that traffic and crowding may be made endogenous. Unlike the macroeconomic model builders, we have the significant advantage of being able to generate many different large sample data bases at relatively low cost.

At any rate, at this point, the inferential methods of either the single equation or multiple equation variety would appear to require considerable research effort. Luckily, unlike many consumer decisions, mode choice does not appear to be one in which, in general, consumers have reason to hide their true feelings.

This view is supported by the fact that our results are quite similar to attitudinal studies which measure importances directly rather than inferring them via statistical inference procedures. Moreover, the difference in costs and time involved in the two approaches is enormous. Hence, it would appear reasonable for transportation planners to rely more heavily on the attitudinal approach to importance estimation. Methods such as projective techniques have been used with apparent success in the past when researchers felt that real attitudes were, or could be, clouded by emotional issues. In fact, given the current uncertainties associated with the inferential approach, it would seem appropriate that it always be complimented with a comparable attitudinal approach.

Vol. 59: J. A. Hanson, Growth in Open Economics. IV, 127 pages. 4°. 1971. DM 16,–

Vol. 60: H. Hauptmann, Schätz- und Kontrolltheorie in stetigen dynamischen Wirtschaftsmodellen. V, 104 Seiten. 4°. 1971. DM 16,–

Vol. 61: K. H. F. Meyer, Wartesysteme mit variabler Bearbeitungsrate. VII, 314 Seiten. 4°. 1971. DM 24,–

Vol. 62: W. Krelle u. G. Gabisch unter Mitarbeit von J. Burgermeister, Wachstumstheorie. VII, 223 Seiten. 4°. 1972. DM 20,–

Vol. 63: J. Kohlas, Monte Carlo Simulation im Operations Research. VI, 162 Seiten. 4°. 1972. DM 16,–

Vol. 64: P. Gessner u. K. Spremann, Optimierung in Funktionenräumen. IV, 120 Seiten. 4°. 1972. DM 16,–

Vol. 65: W. Everling, Exercises in Computer Systems Analysis. VIII, 184 pages. 4°. 1972. DM 18,–

Vol. 66: F. Bauer, P. Garabedian and D. Korn, Supercritical Wing Sections. V, 211 pages. 4°. 1972. DM 20,–

Vol. 67: I. V. Girsanov, Lectures on Mathematical Theory of Extremum Problems. V, 136 pages. 4°. 1972. DM 16,–

Vol. 68: J. Loeckx, Computability and Decidability. An Introduction for Students of Computer Science. VI, 76 pages. 4°. 1972. DM 16,–

Vol. 69: S. Ashour, Sequencing Theory. V, 133 pages. 4°. 1972. DM 16,–

Vol. 70: J. P. Brown, The Economic Effects of Floods. Investigations of a Stochastic Model of Rational Investment Behavior in the Face of Floods. V, 87 pages. 4°. 1972. DM 16,–

Vol. 71: R. Henn und O. Opitz, Konsum- und Produktionstheorie II. V, 134 Seiten. 4°. 1972. DM 16,–

Vol. 72: T. P. Bagchi and J. G. C. Templeton, Numerical Methods in Markov Chains and Bulk Queues. XI, 89 pages. 4°. 1972. DM 16,–

Vol. 73: H. Kiendl, Suboptimale Regler mit abschnittweise linearer Struktur. VI, 146 Seiten. 4°. 1972. DM 16,–

Vol. 74: F. Pokropp, Aggregation von Produktionsfunktionen. VI, 107 Seiten. 4°. 1972. DM 16,–

Vol. 75: GI-Gesellschaft für Informatik e.V. Bericht Nr. 3. 1. Fachtagung über Programmiersprachen · München, 9–11. März 1971. Herausgegeben im Auftag der Gesellschaft für Informatik von H. Langmaack und M. Paul. VII, 280 Seiten. 4°. 1972. DM 24,–

Vol. 76: G. Fandel, Optimale Entscheidung bei mehrfacher Zielsetzung. 121 Seiten. 4°. 1972. DM 16,–

Vol. 77: A. Auslender, Problemes de Minimax via l'Analyse Convexe et les Inégalités Variationnelles: Théorie et Algorithmes. VII, 132 pages. 4°. 1972. DM 16,–

Vol. 78: GI-Gesellschaft für Informatik e.V. 2. Jahrestagung, Karlsruhe, 2.–4. Oktober 1972. Herausgegeben im Auftrag der Gesellschaft für Informatik von P. Deussen. XI, 576 Seiten. 4°. 1973. DM 36,–

Vol. 79: A. Berman, Cones, Matrices and Mathematical Programming. V, 96 pages. 4°. 1973. DM 16,–

Vol. 80: International Seminar on Trends in Mathematical Modelling, Venice, 13–18 December 1971. Edited by N. Hawkes. VI, 288 pages. 4°. 1973. DM 24,–

Vol. 81: Advanced Course on Software Engineering. Edited by F. L. Bauer. XII, 545 pages. 4°. 1973. DM 32,–

Vol. 82: R. Saeks, Resolution Space, Operators and Systems. X, 267 pages. 4°. 1973. DM 22,–

Vol. 83: NTG/GI-Gesellschaft für Informatik, Nachrichtentechnische Gesellschaft. Fachtagung „Cognitive Verfahren und Systeme", Hamburg, 11.–13. April 1973. Herausgegeben im Auftrag der NTG/GI von Th. Einsele, W. Giloi und H.-H. Nagel. VIII, 373 Seiten. 4°. 1973. DM 28,–

Vol. 84: A. V. Balakrishnan, Stochastic Differential Systems I. Filtering and Control. A Function Space Approach. V, 252 pages. 4°. 1973. DM 22,–

Vol. 85: T. Page, Economics of Involuntary Transfers: A Unified Approach to Pollution and Congestion Externalities. XI, 159 pages. 4°. 1973. DM 18,–

Vol. 86: Symposium on the Theory of Scheduling and Its Applications. Edited by S. E. Elmaghraby. VIII, 437 pages. 4°. 1973. DM 32,–

Vol. 87: G. F. Newell, Approximate Stochastic Behavior of n-Server Service Systems with Large n. VIII, 118 pages. 4°. 1973. DM 16,–

Vol. 88: H. Steckhan, Güterströme in Netzen. VII, 134 Seiten. 4°. 1973. DM 16,–

Vol. 89: J. P. Wallace and A. Sherret, Estimation of Product Attributes and Their Importances. V, 94 pages. 4°. 1973. DM 16,–

GPSR Compliance

The European Union's (EU) General Product Safety Regulation (GPSR) is a set of rules that requires consumer products to be safe and our obligations to ensure this.

If you have any concerns about our products, you can contact us on ProductSafety@springernature.com

In case Publisher is established outside the EU, the EU authorized representative is:

Springer Nature Customer Service Center GmbH
Europaplatz 3
69115 Heidelberg, Germany

Batch number: 10844827

Printed by Printforce, the Netherlands